Problem Solving and Critical Thinking for Designers

Christine M. Piotrowski, FASID, IIDA

WILEY

JOHN WILEY & SONS, INC.

Published by John Wiley & Sons, Inc., Hoboken, New Jersey
Published simultaneously in Canada

For general information about our other products and services, please contact our Customer Care Department within the United States at (800) 762-2974, outside the United States at (317) 572-3993 or fax (317) 572-4002.

Wiley also publishes its books in a variety of electronic formats. Some content that appears in print may not be available in electronic books. For more information about Wiley products, visit our web site at www.wiley.com.

Library of Congress Cataloging-in-Publication Data:

Piotrowski, Christine M., 1947-
 Problem solving and critical thinking for designers/
 Christine M. Piotrowski.
  p. cm.
 Includes index.
 ISBN 978-0-470-53671-1 (pbk.); ISBN 978-0-470-95105-7 (ebk.);
 ISBN 978-0-470-95122-4 (ebk.); ISBN 978-1-118-01562-9 (ebk.);
 ISBN 978-1-118-01563-6 (ebk.); ISBN 978-1-118-01564-3 (ebk.)
 1. Architectural design–Decision making–Problems, exercises, etc.
 2. Interior architecture–Decision making–Problems, exercises, etc. I. Title.
 NA2750.P54 2011
 729–dc22   2010043328
Printed in the United States of America

10 9 8 7 6 5

I dedicate this book to my nieces Julie and Jennifer who as wives, mothers, and professionals think critically, problem solve, and make decisions every day.

"If you already know what you are after, there is usually not much point in looking."
　　　　　　　　　　　—Tim Brown, *Change by Design*

Contents

Preface

Do you know what you should do when the husband and wife give conflicting opinions—and approvals—to design suggestions? Is climate change of significant importance to you so that you should become more involved in a practice focused on sustainable design? What will you consider when you next vote for a president? How can you design a facility to be comforting and functional to provide medical treatment for cancer patients?

These dissimilar questions in one way or another relate to the essence of this book. They are situations and dilemmas that will require your skills in problem solving, critical thinking, and decision making. Improving these skills makes you a more sought-after employee and designer, effective business owner, and fulfilled individual.

The interior design profession requires effective problem solving and critical thinking, as they impact all phases of the design project and most work activities of the interior designer. Whether you are a student or professional designer, much of what you do involves these skills. Although most of us do not even think about what we do in terms of these activities, they are a constant part of design. They are also skills that you must perform successfully outside your professional career.

The creation of interiors happens because of the designer's application of design knowledge and skills to solving the problem presented by the client. The creation of an interior that satisfies and thrills a homeowner, wows guests of a new restaurant, comforts patients in medical spaces, and helps all sorts of other businesses achieve their business goals does not happen simply because a designer has applied memorized facts about design to the project.

Several years ago I took some business classes, and one of the professors made an indelible impression on me. He taught us that there was no one right, absolute answer to almost anything in business. There is a process, of course, of thinking through the problem in most cases, but often there was more than one way to get to an acceptable answer.

That is, of course, true of interior design as well. There are few absolute ways to design any space or interior. The solutions and "right answers" vary greatly by the actors involved in the drama of design. Two designers given the same parameters and goals for the same project will always come up with two different solutions. It is actually one of the beauties of the profession. Getting there happens from acquiring an enormous amount of techniques, information, and skills in order to design any type of interior space in the 21st century. Getting there also involves mastering the art of problem solving, using critical thinking, and learning how to make decisions.

Employers have been clamoring for "thinking" designers. Design firm owners talk constantly about their experiences with the newest generation of professionals. They chat about how they

have many positive attributes, yet the less experienced professionals have a hard time performing comprehensive problem
solving and critical thinking. To be honest, it is not just the newest
professional who lacks these skills. Many designers have forgotten how the process of problem solving makes a positive impact
on the effective progression of a project from initial programming through the final installation.

Based on numerous comments and discussions with educators
and professionals, this book will help both the student and professional designer find concise information to help them increase
problem solving and decision making skills. The reader will explore topics that are essential to finding effective success regardless of one's position in the industry. Although the examples are
primarily those related to interior design, other design professionals will find much relevant material to apply to their design
specialty.

Let's be clear—this is not another book about how to do programming or basic space planning. Chapters 1 and 2 present an
overview of critical thinking and its importance to the interior
designer. Chapter 2 highlights a discussion about for whom we
really design and tips on using time effectively. It also includes a
brief discussion on an important new business model referred
to as design thinking. This fascinating subject has stood the
business community on its ear in recent years, and it is important for designers to understand how it might impact the design
profession.

The next four chapters present design problem solving starting
with defining the problem to the process of reaching a decision. Chapter 3 discusses project and business goal development
and problem definition and concept statements. Chapter 4 then
moves to discussing the topic of asking questions. Included in this

chapter are sections on ways to improve listening skills, avoiding disputes, and negotiation techniques. In Chapter 5, the discussion focuses on "looking for answers" or the process used to conduct research to develop facts and explore a research project. Chapter 5 also includes an overview of evidence-based design and a section on assessing information from the Internet. Chapter 6 brings the problem-solving process to a conclusion with a discussion on the decision-making process and strategies useful in making decisions.

The final chapter looks at decision making with a different eye as it explores ethical decision making. The ethical misdeeds of individuals reported in the media, and the ethical misdeeds of designers as well, make clients think twice about trusting their interior designer. Topics include how ethics and business can be in conflict and what clients expect from designers.

Each chapter concludes with a series of items and cases for discussion. Instructors may choose to use these for class discussion or written assignments. Professionals will find these thought provoking, as many are situations shared with me by other designers. Like all case study methodology, they are for discussion, and as such do not have absolute answers. One might say they encourage the Socratic method of teaching rather than a more traditional approach of lecture. There may be many "right" answers, just as design rarely has an absolute answer to any design project.

I look forward to feedback on the lively discussions that will undoubtedly ensue.

Acknowledgments

When asked by my editor to do this book, I found the idea intriguing. I started my research about critical thinking by having conversations with numerous designers and educators. I became convinced that it was a topic that needed a platform. To all those peers who answered my questions, thank you for your input and encouragement. Thank you also to John Martin-Rutherford, who had a very positive conversation with my editor and me as we contemplated this project.

I need to thank my friends and family for being very understanding of my moods and stress during this project. It goes without saying that the interior design community has been very gracious to me over the years, and I could not have done this book without the support and friendship of peers. I feel truly blessed that this book became a reality and could not have been done it without all of their support.

I want to specifically acknowledge those individuals who were kind enough to read chapter drafts or provide reviews. They helped me fine-tune chapter topics and recommended a few I hadn't thought of. Their suggestions helped tremendously. Thank you to Judith Fosshage, FASID, IIDA; Carol Morrow, PhD, ASID,

IDEC; Charlene Conrad, IDC, IDNS; Dru Lawlor, FASID; Suzan Globus, FASID; Sybil Jane Barrido, ASID; Robin Wagner, ASID; Greta Guelich, ASID; Barbara Robbins; and Bob Krikac, ASID, IDEC.

Of course, I also want to acknowledge the designers who provided short articles, illustrations, and graphics—sometimes on very short notice. My thanks goes out to Laurie Smith, ASID; Lisa Whited, IIDA, ASID; Caren Martin, PhD, FASID, IDEC; Sybil Jane Barrido, ASID; and Shannon Harris. Thank you, Suzan Globus, FASID; Robert Wright, FASID; Michael Thomas, FASID, CAPS; Rosalyn Cama, FASID; and Mary Knott, Allied Member ASID, CAPS, for once again letting me take advantage of your expertise. In addition, I wish to acknowledge Michael Berens and the American Society of Interior Designers and editor Meg Portillo at the *Journal of Interior Design* for providing material and permission to publish important illustrations.

Thank you as well to all those students and grads—part of the millennium generation that inspired this book. You have a lot to give to us old-timers, just as we have a lot to share with you. Let's move forward to a mutually beneficial relationship!

Finally, I would like to give a special acknowledgment and thanks to Paul Drougas, my editor for this book and good friend at John Wiley & Sons. His patience, support, and encouragement in asking me to write on this topic and see it to completion has been an amazing gift. I also want to thank Sadie Abuhoff, editorial assistant at John Wiley, who once again has gone above and beyond, as well as all the production folks at John Wiley.

Thinking Critically

In September 2008, the banking industry nearly failed in the United States, resulting in a massive worldwide recession. Some predicted that the economy would take years to recover. What does this have to do with the interior design profession and learning how to *think critically*?

The design and construction industry were particularly hard hit. Homeowners lost their homes to foreclosures. Builders lost the opportunity to obtain credit for construction loans. Many companies went out of business, reducing opportunities for commercial design work. Thousands in the design/build industry lost their jobs or their businesses. Interior designers and design firm owners were faced with critical decisions about how to operate during this challenging time.

Developing critical thinking skills is essential in the complex world we live in today. It is a necessary skill in both your professional and personal life. Thinking critically is what design business owners, practitioners, industry members, and students must do to sustain their positions in the industry through good times as well as bad. Every day you must make sense of what is happening amidst an onslaught of information via the media. Who to believe? Who has the "correct" information and ideas? Design professionals must think critically to design projects for clients, grow professionally, and make critical personal decisions. Design firms fail even in good economic conditions.

Thinking critically impacts design decisions made during the project process, the operation of a design practice, and personal decisions. What codes impact the design of an interior? What is the best way to evaluate products that claim to be sustainable? How should a business owner set up design contracts to ensure that the client will pay his bills? How do you know that the information on which you rely is accurate? Where did the information come from?

Answering questions such as these will require thinking critically, as there are few easy answers anymore. The world and the design profession have become incredibly complex. You are bombarded with information from numerous sources. Thinking critically is a vital skill in your daily life and your profession. As you will see, thinking critically impacts many of the tasks associated with the interior design process.

WHAT IS CRITICAL THINKING?

Critical thinking is highly valued by the business community, including, of course, the design professions. Students, entry-level, and practicing designers need to learn to think more carefully and critically. Thinking critically impacts you in many ways, including determining client needs, solving difficult space plans, making business decisions, and dealing with clients and others with interests in the project.

So what is critical thinking? *Critical thinking* "consists of an awareness of a set of interrelated critical questions, plus the ability and willingness to ask and answer them at appropriate times."[1] It is thinking oriented toward consideration, evaluation, and the synthesis of information, resulting in a decision. It helps you in all sorts of decision-making scenarios and involves:

- Asking appropriate questions
- Sorting out information
- Evaluating options
- Making an informed decision

Of course, not all thinking is critical thinking. When your mind is in "operation," you are *thinking*, which essentially is active use of your brain. When you decide where to go to lunch, you are engaging in thinking. Agreeing on which events to schedule for the association you belong to involves thinking. Determining which products you would like to specify for a project involves thinking. Of course, some may argue that these examples also represent critical thinking.

You likely will be involved in many issues that will require your ability to problem solve and think through what is happening around you. Making sense about what is going on in the larger scheme of things is important to the interior designer. Events and decisions by others impact the profession and what goes on beyond an individual's immediate world. Understanding that outside world is central to today's successful professional.

Critical thinking should not be thought of as criticism or something that is negative in connotation. When you think critically, you are not being asked to find fault with the subject at hand, nor is it assumed that you are looking to do so. Criticism is very different from thinking critically. More about this perception appears later in this chapter.

WHO IS A CRITICAL THINKER?

Developing critical thinking skills will help make you a more valuable employee and a more prudent individual. Are you clear about how the legislation of design practice (or the lack of it) impacts your work as an interior designer in your jurisdiction? What will you do when you are certain a colleague behaves unethically? Are you concerned about the lack of direction on the environment? Maybe right now you are thinking only about how to complete the project you were recently assigned in studio or whether to go out with friends this weekend.

Your complex world requires you to seek information and make decisions beyond the most obvious. Your great grandparents didn't have a lot of choices on many of the things that you take for granted today. Deciding where to go to for groceries is an example. If the neighborhood store didn't have it, your great grandparents didn't get it. Today, there are numerous options, with huge selections of products to purchase. Because of this, even which store to frequent involves thinking critically.

Designers are critical thinkers because the many decisions that are made during the process of designing an interior and operating a business are not simple. The vast majority of those decisions directly impact clients and users of interiors. That in itself is an awesome responsibility. Making a wrong choice on fabrics, for example, can affect the health, safety, and welfare of the clients and other users of interiors. Violating local laws by deciding not to obtain required licenses impacts the individual, her business, and her professional standing—and the client.

Critical Thinking Behavior

Someone who is a critical thinker has some basic behaviors. Many behaviors might have been cultivated from childhood. Yet all can be developed over time. Here are several basic characteristics of a critical thinker:

- Be inquisitive and always be open to learning.
- Don't be afraid to ask questions.
- Don't feel self-conscious when you don't know something.
- Objectively evaluate information.
- Don't accept information on face value.
- Realize that quick decisions are rarely correct.

The last one is particularly important in this fast-paced world. Even though they are often demanded, quick conclusions or solutions are rarely the best answer. For example, text message code is easy for young designers to understand. These same messages confuse and frustrate older designers and clients. In the same vein, the first floor plan that seems to work is rarely the best solution. Additional solutions can result in space savings, better traffic paths, or room for more employees.

By becoming a critical thinker, a designer seeks to ask questions about the task or situation beyond previously learned experiences and beliefs. This is true whether it involves a professional issue or a personal one. The goal is to arrive at carefully considered options rather than jumping to quick conclusions.

THE IMPORTANCE OF THINKING CRITICALLY IN INTERIOR DESIGN

Your ability to think critically may be as important to your job as your creative skills. Many readers might argue this. However, time and again, employers and educators queried about this important topic report critical thinking as a crucial skill that designers must have in the modern design world.

Solutions to the problems involved in designing any type of interior space are not easy. Professional designers must consider a huge assortment of criteria beyond the stereotypical "picking out colors and fabrics." Sustainable design, accessibility, product specifications, building codes, the internal environment, the client's preferences and needs, and on and on, are criteria important in all projects today. Business practices are also impacted. For example, the manner in which the client is charged, accurate financial accounting, legal responsibilities, and employee relations all influence the continued life of a design firm.

On the job, critical thinking helps the designer when faced with objections by the client. Through the course of the project the designer has researched many issues and tried many approaches to the design problem. He or she has evaluated these approaches before presenting them to the client. Finally, the designer is able to present the best alternatives and reduce the impact of emotional decision making. Yet the client might object to the plan, the fabrics, color scheme, or any number of other items and issues related to the project. The designer must step back and critically think and problem solve to move the project along.

Interior design requires complex decisions with the necessity of determining choices that might be ideal, workable, and reasonable. This is commonly due to the budget. A client might desire to have an incredibly designed home with all the best furniture and finishes—the "ideal" great home. The budget just will not handle the costs. A restaurateur may fall in love with design ideas that are "over the top" but can't handle the extra expenses. The designer's job is to help the client achieve the ideal workable and reasonable solution even when the dollars are not available for buying the very best. Being able to think critically helps the designer solve these crucial problems.

Every day, designers must consider information provided by numerous individuals involved in a design project. The information is not always objective. A client might not disclose that the couple is about to get a divorce or the business is on the verge of bankruptcy. A vendor may influence the specification of a particular project based on price increases rather than the item being the "best" for the project.

How do you evaluate the information provided by others? By asking questions, being observant, and evaluating the information related to the needs of the project and client. Thinking critically helps you keep the project on a profitable and effective track.

Creative Thinking

Creativity and *creative thinking* is imagining something new from something that already exists. It is looking for new ways to do something, new answers, or simply changing what exists in one context to a different context that is hopefully better. It might be astonishingly new, as some might say the Apple iPod was when first introduced, or something that is simply better than it was, such as a kitchen remodeled for someone suddenly permanently in a wheelchair.

Creativity is not the same thing as being "artistic." Some very creative people say they couldn't draw a stick figure, let alone produce a painting. Yet they create new products and new solutions to old problems, solve difficult business challenges,

(continued)

and yes, design interiors. Interior designers naturally consider themselves to be creative thinkers. The purpose of design, they are often told, is to create. Creative thinking is certainly essential to interior design problem solving.

Creative thinking is not the same as critical thinking. Critical thinking involves analyzing and planning and is quite objective in focus. Critical thinking also encourages the application of logic and left-brained thinking. Creative thinking encourages willingness to change and see things differently, generating new ideas and flexibility. It is subjective in focus and is quite right-brained.

Naturally, creative thinking is important for interior designers to solve the problems of their clients. Critical thinking is necessary to analyze and evaluate information that is received from clients, vendors, colleagues, and stakeholders to a project. Today's complex world needs designers and employees in general who have the ability to be comfortable in both worlds.

IT IS NOT CRITICISM

One thing that thinking critically does not involve is criticism. Students are familiar with the concept of criticism, since studio projects are regularly criticized and graded by instructors. When a "crit" occurs, instructors are trying to determine how well the student has accomplished the required tasks and makes objective judgments on the design interpretations.

Let's be clear as to what *criticism* is by looking at a dictionary definition of the word: "criticism: the expression of disapproval of someone or something based on perceived faults or mistakes."[2]

Criticism of or by leaders, managers, clients, and even peers is not what thinking critically is about. Disapproving of the client's ideas about design might be something you would criticize, but it is not critical thinking. Not being in favor of legislation for interior design practice might be criticism of the concept, but again, it is not the same thing as engaging in a meaningful discussion and thinking critically about the pros and cons of legislation.

Criticism can also end up being mean-spirited, even hurtful. That hurt can come directly from the words used by the person making the criticism or be an internal effect on the recipient. "Sally did a terrible job of presenting to the client," said one design colleague to another. Sally may already feel awful because she knew deep down that she had really blown the presentation.

To repeat, critical thinking is not criticism. It is thinking clearly. It is considering facts. It is looking at options and determining the best course of action or in other ways to make a decision or take a stand.

CONCLUSION

Developing critical thinking skills is essential for design professionals in today's complex world. Obtaining an education in design, learning the skills required in the profession, and gaining an appreciation for the art of design, as well as learning the vast amount and kinds of technical information that apply to design are naturally all very important. They are among the tools that the professional designer needs to critically solve problems for clients. It makes little difference (other than scale, perhaps) whether the project is a large (or small) private residence, hotel, office, or other type of commercial space. Thinking critically expands the designer's value to clients, improves business performance, and indeed makes a better citizen.

FOR DISCUSSION

These discussion items and scenario cases require you to use critical thinking to solve one or more problems. In many of these items and cases, you must take the role of a design practice business owner or a practicing designer. There is no *one* right answer to any of these discussion items or scenarios.

1. List some ways critical thinking impacts the work of an interior designer involved in a residential project; a restaurant project.

2. Describe an interaction with a client and designer where critical thinking is necessary to avoid an argument with the client.

3. Explain a situation where you were reluctant to ask one or more questions to clarify an issue or statement you didn't understand (or disagreed with). Was this a person in authority such as a boss or professor? Would that have changed your reluctance at all?

4. Designers are constantly forced to make choices in the products they specify for a client. Locate information and two different fabric samples suitable for seating in a model for an assisted living apartment. Decide which items you think will give the best wear for the use. Be prepared to discuss why you are choosing this item.

5. Try to re-create the decision you made that resulted in the purchase of an expensive item such as a television, computer, or car. What was the process you used to come to the decision you made? Whom did you ask for help? What factors impacted your decision to buy the item you purchased?

Cases for Discussion

1. A man walks into your showroom (or studio) and begins handling expensive accessory items you have displayed. He is dressed in denims that are dusty and dirty, a dirty-looking T-shirt covered by an unbuttoned long-sleeved shirt, and sandals. His hair is mussed, and he has what appears to be a three-day growth of beard. He says, "I'm looking for some crystal items to give to my mother for her birthday. I want something expensive, as it is her 75th birthday."

   ■ How would you greet this individual? What would your impression of him be?

2. Beverly and Todd are the owners of a six-person interior design firm in a West Coast city. They specialize in high-end residential work, but also have occasionally obtained projects for office spaces. Beverly and Todd have about 25 percent of their studio organized as a retail display space.

   They have spent a combined 65 hours over the last three weeks preparing sketches and preliminary product specifications for a residence for a celebrity. The contractor and architect need approved design development drawings and materials finishes within three days to keep the project on schedule. Keeping on schedule is a critical issue for the client.

   The designers have met with the client several times, as well as the client's assistant, since they began the project three months ago. During those meetings, they obtained approvals on the project ideas and proposed products.

   The client and her assistant have scheduled a meeting with the designers for this evening. The purpose of the meeting is for a final review of sketches, drawings, and specifications. Earlier today, Beverly told the architect she expected to get the approvals later today. The architect emailed the contractor to go ahead with the drywall prep work for the wall coverings that Beverly said were being proposed.

That evening, the client came in and out of the meeting (at the client's hotel suite), leaving the discussions to the assistant. Finally, the client sat down and looked at all the samples and screamed, "What the heck are you trying to do to my reputation! This will be hideous! Didn't you hear anything I said during all those other times we talked?"

- What are the issues involved in this case?
- You are Beverly (or Todd). What will you do to resolve this sudden turn of events?
- What information is missing to help you decide what to do?

3. Glenda and John are both very competitive in class. John always gets better grades than Glenda on studio projects. One day, John left his laptop on his desk to go to the sample room to get some fabric items. While he was gone, Glenda looked through his files for the project they were working on. She saw a very creative solution to the part of the project that she was having a lot of difficulty with. She made a fast drawing of the solution and subsequently used the essential elements of that idea in her project. There were two other people in the studio at the time who saw Glenda look at John's laptop.

- If you were one of the other people in the room at this time, what would you do?

NOTES

1. M. Neil Browne and Stuart M. Keeley, *Asking the Right Questions,* 7th ed. (Upper Saddle River, NJ: Pearson/Prentice Hall, 2007), 3.
2. *The Oxford American College Dictionary* (New York: Oxford University Press, 2002), 325.

2

Design as Process

Honestly, didn't you first think that the interior design profession simply involved creativity and designing beautiful interiors? Whether you are a student or professional, you have discovered that creativity is only part of the requirements of the design professional.

Certainly, the work of the designer is creative. A big reason many clients hire interior designers is for their creative skills. However, interior design is also a profession that requires thinking critically, problem solving, and decision making, as well as creativity. Some might say that these skills are the primary responsibility and pursuit of the interior designer.

Design work involves looking for solutions to problems. What do I mean by *problem?* A problem is some difficulty that needs to be solved. It might be the relatively simple problem of helping a client select accessories or something more complex, such as the interior planning and executing of a mega hotel or cancer treatment center.

In order to solve interior design problems, designers use a process. The *design process* is often described as an orderly arrangement of phases or steps. Yet designers should not think of these steps as having absolute start and stop points. Not all projects require a designer to go through all the steps, but most benefit from following the process. A process is a good thing—even in a creative profession.

Each phase also requires thinking critically, working to solve the problem, and making decisions to complete the project. The knowledge gained in academic programs provides a foundation for these skills in design. Academic preparation and experience provide the designer the background needed to perform the tasks of the interior designer. Nevertheless, design problems don't always become resolved due to the application of memorized knowledge and skills developed in the academic setting. Many solutions to problems require more thought. That's where critical thinking once again comes into play. Designers have to think critically and carefully in order solve design problems. The skills and techniques used to think critically are used to resolve many problems posed by the parameters of the design project.

THE DESIGN PROCESS—A BRIEF REVIEW

The design process involves numerous activities and tasks to bring about a solution. Some involve working with clients and others involved in the project. Some tasks require the preparation of graphic documents, such as floor plans and perspectives. Other tasks include researching information, such as applicable codes. And, of course, tasks also involve critical thinking, problem solving, and decision making.

Design problems for the interior designer involve all areas of design practice, such as planning and design, product specification, working with others, business practices, and professional issues. Problems naturally arise in all phases of a project.

Following a process ensures that everything that must be done is taken care of, details are not missed, and the project moves smoothly from beginning to end. A process is also necessary, since not all projects are completed by a sole designer. Many are produced by a team of designers working under the direction of a project designer who will oversee the team.

The design process, then, is *design problem solving*. It deals with achieving a solution to whatever the client's problem happens to be. When the client has a problem, he or she might express the problem as a need, since most don't like to admit they have "problems." Here are a couple of quick examples: "I need a more functional arrangement of my store"; "I need furniture for my vacation home in Aspen." Perhaps it is expressed as a want: "I want my dental suite to help make the patients feel comfortable"; "I want the job done on time, on budget, and no excuses."

Problem solving through the design process involves several steps grouped by analysis and synthesis, as shown in Table 2.1. *Analysis* in design involves obtaining, reviewing, and clarifying information and setting goals. *Synthesis* in design involves bringing all the information and other tasks together to form a solution to

TABLE 2.1. Differences between Analysis and Synthesis

Analysis	Synthesis
Define the problem	Develop alternate solutions
Establish goals	Evaluate the alternative solutions
Gather information	Select and present the best option
Analyze the problem	Obtain approval from client
Implement the agreed-upon solution	Evaluate the project solution and success

Adapted from Rosemary Kilmer and W. Otie Kilmer, *Designing Interiors* (Fort Worth, TX: Harcourt Brace Jovanovich, 1992), 158–159.

the problem. The tasks involved in the analysis step are primarily the phases of predesign and programming. The tasks involved in synthesis are those of schematic design, design development, contract documents, and contract administration. You will see in Chapter 3 that the items in Table 2.1 closely resemble the steps in the basic problem-solving and decision-making processes. In-depth discussions of these concepts and steps are provided in subsequent chapters.

As for the design process itself, it has been recognized to involve five phases, with many tasks in each phase. As a quick overview, a brief description of those phases is included. There are many sources for detailed information on the tasks included in each phase. Several sources are listed in the references. Since this book is about critical thinking and problem solving, the remainder of this chapter will look at some issues that are important to discuss beyond the actual tasks of design.

Programming is considered the information-gathering phase. The designer seeks to obtain as much information as possible concerning the responsibilities outlined in the scope of services. Depending on the project, information will be gathered from the client, employees, project architect, municipal departments (regarding codes), and others as might be needed.

Schematic design is where preliminary planning and early decision making takes place. Bubble diagrams, adjacency diagrams, and concept sketches are common visual documents. In addition, the designer prepares design concept statements, and makes preliminary product selections.

Design development is the stage where the designer finalizes with the client many decisions concerning the project. For example, the designer will detail floor plans to ensure that space plans will work, furniture will fit, and codes will be met. The designer must also be sure that the *furniture, furnishings, and equipment (FF&E)* plan items are available and meet client needs.

Contract documents are the construction and installation drawings, specifications, and other required documents needed to get the project built and installed. Dimensioned floor plans, lighting/ reflected ceiling plans, FF&E, and finish schedules represent some of these items. Drawings often need to be coordinated with the project architect and contractors who will also be involved in completing the building installation of the project.

Contract administration involves the competitive bidding or placing of orders for the work and items to be built and installed. Competitive bidding commonly occurs for commercial projects, such as offices. For smaller projects and many residential projects, the designer might be responsible for procuring the goods and services needed to complete the project.

The "Project Assessment Planning" tool on pages 17 to 19 provides an approach to preparing for the programming and subsequent planning assessment to design a project—in this case, a kitchen. It shows how critical thinking plays an important part in the gathering of information needed for a design project.

Project Assessment Planning: An Example of Program Questioning Preparation

Provided by: Mary Fisher Knott, CID, Allied Member ASID, CAPS. Mary Fisher Designs. Scottsdale, AZ

Developing a cohesive design for a kitchen featuring ergonomic applications requires several steps in the planning and concept stages.

1. Establish the goal of the final design. Interview the client and gather visual information of their design preferences.

(continued)

The initial interview of the client to establish their priorities and expectations is just as important as the physical characteristics of the space to be planned.

2. Assess the client's physical characteristics relating to access and movement within the space.

   Planning a space ergonomically involves observation of the client's ability to move within the area as well as measuring their ability to access spaces within the room.

3. Define the cooking skills of the client.

   The cooking skills of the client influence the appliance and plumbing fixture selection, cabinet placement and storage, and counter heights, as well as cooking utensil assortment.

4. Research and select appliances and fixtures that match the abilities of the client.

   The specification of appliances and plumbing fixtures that match a client's cooking skill offers the client elements fit to their cooking needs without burdening them with features they will never use.

5. Analyze storage and cabinet needs.

   Storage systems can be planned that offer cookware and utensils at the cook's first point of use.

6. Define aesthetic and functional design criteria.

   Establishing the style and task areas of the kitchen must be done early in the design process.

7. Develop a space plan that meets aesthetic and functional criteria.

   When furniture is included in the design of the kitchen, the designation of social and task areas in the space must be made.

8. Develop the decorative scheme of the space.

   Attention given to detail work at all stages of the design most often results in a successful completion of the space.

9. Prepare specifications for the project.

> The more detailed your specifications, the better the communication will be with contractors, subcontractors, and artisans. Never assume they understand.

FOR WHOM DO WE DESIGN?

Students have an especially difficult time understanding that design, while a creative endeavor, is not a personal expression of creativity. Professional designers sometimes forget that the client has a lot to say about what will happen in solving the design problem. It is not a profession, such as painting, sculpture, and other fine arts, where the artist is free to create from his or her head without thought of pleasing others. Interior design services are executed for clients. If there are no clients, there is no work for the interior designer.

Instructors place requirements on projects since that is similar to what will happen in the "real world." Interior design clients impose their wishes, needs, and wants on a project more times than not. Client needs and feelings impact whether the interior will be a creative expression or a purely functional solution. Whether designers like it or not, those needs and wants often limit the creative expressions of the designer.

Of course, clients want the creative expertise that designers bring to a project. The lessons learned, skills mastered, and knowledge obtained are all important criteria the client inquires about when hiring a designer. The client is expecting the designer to utilize all of these to offer effective, practical, and creative ways of enhancing the aesthetics and function of interiors.

Clients do indeed hire interior designers to help them achieve that "beautiful" home, office complex, restaurant, or whatever the space. But many clients are not concerned about beauty as much as they might be concerned about function. A retail store needs to be aesthetically pleasing, but it also needs to be a space to help sell whatever the product might be. Is the design of an auto parts dealership beautiful? Perhaps, but the owner is probably more concerned about functions and display of merchandise than the design's winning an award. Some parts of the office complex need to be aesthetically pleasing, but providing the work spaces for employees to achieve their job responsibilities is often more important than creating a "beautiful" space. A beautiful space that does not work functionally is not a successful interior as far as the client is concerned.

Of course, your passions, experience, and innate ability in the profession enter into the project. Your knowledge of design elements and principles, color, structures, and all the other parts and pieces that are utilized to create an interior space enters into any design solution. That is what gives uniqueness to each solution. That individual perspective on how to solve a project is why each solution to a project in a class is somewhat different from every other one.

It is true that school projects are in part designed for the professor. That does not mean that he or she has a preconceived idea of what the project should look like. Professors by and large evaluate projects based not on their own conception of what a project should look like, but on such things as:

- Meeting functional needs.
- Building and life safety codes.
- Technical accuracy.
- Workable floor plans and furniture layouts.
- Color schemes suitable to the project requirements.
- Use of design elements and principles.

In the so-called real world, a project also must meet these types of requirements, though the client has not likely expressed them as such during programming. Professional projects often must be designed to "please" individuals other than the client who signed the contract. These other individuals are called *stakeholders*—the various people or groups that have an interest in a project. For a residence, the stakeholders are simple enough—the homeowner is the client and the person who primarily must be pleased with our ideas. But there can be others directly or indirectly involved in the decisions for a residence. In commercial design, we think of the client as the restaurant owner or the doctor whose practice will house the medical suite. A commercial space also has multiple stakeholders that will have influence on the ultimate design of the interior of a commercial space. Table 2.2 provides a list of common stakeholders.

The problem for the interior designer is that the wants, needs, ideas, and interests of these varied individuals can easily trump the creative expression the interior designer wishes to impart in the project. Students need to understand that outcomes must

TABLE 2.2. Common Stakeholders Directly or Indirectly Involved in Project Decisions

Resident family members
Relatives and friends
Contractors
Building inspectors
Homeowners' associations (HOAs)
Owner of house or facility
Developer of property
Employees
Guests/customers
Architect and other consultants
Specialists, such as a commercial kitchen designer for a restaurant
Sometimes the spouse or significant other of the commercial property owner

focus on the client, project needs, and requirements. Interior design in the 21st century is not solely about satisfying the designer's personal ego. Satisfying client needs and wants and solving client problems through design solutions is critical to the professional designer.

So the answer to the question and quandary posed at the beginning of this section is that we design for others, not ourselves. We design for the client and others, not ourselves.

Workflow Solutions

By now you understand that interior design has a process to move a project in an orderly fashion from client contact to project completion. To enhance effectiveness, businesses also utilize processes to get the work of the business completed. This can be especially helpful for businesses that manage data or documents. This business concept is called *workflow*.

Workflow helps identify the steps, tasks, or procedures that should be used to handle such things as processes, documents, and information.

The development of workflow and workflow solutions helps to make sense of complex tasks. By thinking through what must be done, steps are laid out in logical order, speeding up efficiency and quality. In design, there are many logical steps that require that one step be accomplished before another is started. For example, scheduling the installation of carpeting or other flooring should not be done until all the wall and ceiling treatments are finished. This simple workflow solution helps prevent damage to the carpeting or other flooring.

Workflow systems and solutions can be used to find new functional solutions to old problems. Interior designers can use this concept to help a client find better ways of working that are actually impacted by the design and layout of spaces. For example, a new way of positioning office cubicles can increase the efficiency of work that must move from one employee or group of employees to others. In order to do this, the interior designer must clearly understand the client's business—the tasks involved, how they do the work, and even the strategic future plans of the business.

Designers can help clients think outside the box of how things have been done to how they can be done better by utilizing workflow solutions and strategies. By doing this, the designer has the potential for developing better client outcomes (which means results) not only in the design of a space but can also impact the actual work of the business. When improved client outcomes can occur from the efforts of the interior designer, the designer has made himself or herself more valuable to the client. This increased value to the client also results in increased potential revenue for the design firm.

Computer software systems can be utilized to enhance workflow systems. Scheduling systems help to keep track of the process of a design project regardless of its simplicity or complexity. Large design firms use project management software to help them with keeping track of the complexity of a project. Individuals can use workflow solutions by following time management practices via the computer—or even manually.

NOT THE FIRST ANSWER

Design problems are never really easy to solve, even for the most experienced professional. Rarely is the first "solution" the best solution. The complexity of design means that movement from point "A" (the problem defined) to point "B" (the solution) is frequently a winding road.

Students today are used to receiving information and making things happen in a hurry. Instant messaging and texting are just two examples of how today's generation has created an innate desire to get to the answer quickly. That usually doesn't work for excellent professional interior design.

Certainly, the competitive nature of the interior design profession demands that solutions come quickly. Since many clients demand "cheaper, better, faster," it has become more common for designers to try to present the first reasonably workable solution. Settling for a fast solution, however, does not necessarily lead to truly creative design. When I was in grad school, one of my professors told the class that the first solution is never the best solution—that it is important to keep searching. Almost all designers know that it is rare for the first solution to be truly the best.

You cannot search forever. You have only so much time to spend on each part of each project. There is always an underlying time limit on how long you can spend finding the best creative solution. There are deadlines to be met and other clients to serve. Experience helps you make better decisions resulting in quicker solutions.

Creative problem solvers and thinkers do not seek merely to determine a fast solution and then make it *the* solution. Exploring for the best solutions is what creative problem solving and thinking are all about. The extra experience of trying more than one solution helps make achieving solutions to other projects quicker. This is how you learn what works and what does not.

Don't settle for your first solution.

USING TIME EFFECTIVELY

I don't know who first said "time is money," but it certainly applies to interior design practice. And the more that can be accomplished in a day, the greater the potential for increased revenue. Learning good time management is important for professionals and students.

Many students find managing time difficult since parents often took care of that task. The boss will expect you to manage your time. He or she will not do it for you. Certainly, multitasking is a skill in which students and graduates who are part of the Millennium generation (those born after 1985) are well versed. In interior design, multitasking often means working on more than one project at a time, not doing more than one task at a time.

Deadlines exist in the academic setting just as they do in the real world. Projects are due on a specific day. Tests are scheduled throughout the semester. Time management involves managing deadlines as well as time.

When you worked on projects in the academic setting, you moved on to other activities when you felt you were done. If the instructor gave you two weeks to complete the project and you felt you were finished in less time, you might move on to other things, perhaps even deciding not to attend class until the project due date. In the working world, you will work on many projects at the same time. The client or the boss gives deadlines. Meeting a deadline early is a good thing if the solution is effective and well done. Meeting a deadline early also means you are ready to do other work—it does not mean you have time off away from the office. Professional interior design is not a race to see who can finish first.

Here are several key time management tips for those who are challenged by finding the time to get everything done:

- A calendar or scheduling software is the starting point.
- Use the calendar to schedule all your work and personal appointments.
- Create a master to-do list of all your assignments, projects, appointments, and tasks.
- Break big tasks down into small parts based on due dates.
- Develop a second to-do list of what must be done each day.
- Include notations on due dates, and coordinate your to-do list with your calendar.
- Prioritize your daily lists so that you are working on the most important items first.
- Less important items each day can then be rescheduled to a later day, if feasible.
- Estimate how long it will take to accomplish each task.
- Check off what has been done to show accomplishment.

If you have not been managing your time very well, it will take some time to develop these new habits. It is important that you keep at it. There is an old saying that it takes 21 days (at least) to develop a new habit. Once in place, you will find yourself able to work more effectively. There are several books listed in the references for more information on time management.

DESIGN THINKING

It seems that businesses at large have finally realized that "design" can mean more than how a space looks or the aesthetics of a product. Businesses are seeing that the process of design can bring innovative thinking to problem solving within the corporate environment. This methodology is called *design thinking*.

David Kelley, the founder of IDEO, a global design and innovation consultancy firm in California, coined the term *design
thinking* in 2003.[1] Companies have used something akin to design thinking for many years through research and development
efforts. Yet, design thinking is a far more innovative approach
to corporate product design than traditional research and
development.

A frequently quoted definition comes from Tim Brown, CEO and
president of IDEO. In a June 2008 *Harvard Business Review* article, Brown defined design thinking as "a discipline that uses the
designer's sensibility and methods to match people's needs with
what is technologically feasible and what a viable business strategy can convert into customer value and market opportunity."[2]
It is a process that helps designers develop innovative design solutions to problems. While the main focus has been on product
development, design thinking can impact the way a business is
organized and potentially has many other applications.

How Does It Work?

Design thinking is about innovation. It involves looking at what
could be. Many times "what could be" a solution results in developing products or other solutions that a consumer might not
even quite realize they want—until they see the new solution.
The Apple iPod is a constant example in the literature. There
were MP3, cassette, and portable CD players before the iPod.
But Apple developed an innovative delivery system (iTunes) to
augment its player. The rest, as they say, is history.

Those who promote design thinking might be a consultancy such
as IDEO hired by large corporations who look to a designer to
solve a problem for them. This is much like an interior designer
is hired to solve a client's interior problems. Design thinking is

also being used within corporations to develop new products or to solve other problems.

A key to design thinking is a shift away from traditional problem-solving methodologies. The design thinking process can feel chaotic to very structured businesses. Creativity and innovation, proponents say, do not come from a formal step-by-step methodology. There are steps in the design thinking process, however.

Tim Brown describes design thinking as a system of spaces rather than a sequence of steps. The spaces that make up the design thinking process can and often do overlap, rather than have distinct beginnings and ends. According to Brown, the three spaces involve "*inspiration*, the problem or opportunity that motivates the search for solutions; *ideation*, the process of generating, developing, and testing ideas; and *implementation*, the path that leads from the project room to the market."[3]

The process begins with what they refer to as a project (not a problem). Work during the inspiration space starts with a project brief developed to set constraints, benchmarks, and objectives. A project team evolves; sometimes people are directed to the team, sometimes people join the team in process. Many times, these project teams are interdisciplinary, involving individuals who can bring specialized knowledge to the project from outside the design team. An example is a health care specialist to help design utensils for people with arthritis.

During the ideation space, the team tries to come up with many ideas to solve the project. These might be very outside the box or rather mundane. The team uses techniques, such as brainstorming and sketching, to come up with many possibilities during ideation. Rough prototyping might come into play at this point with a product. Visuals, such as sketches and prototyping, help the designers see the possibilities.

Naturally, not all possibilities can be developed to the end point of a product or other type of solution. Choices must be made as to which might be the most promising. One or possibly two solutions are refined further, and probably one will be eliminated.

The implementation space necessitates decision making. Whether the new product is a financially viable solution is certainly one question that must be asked of even the most innovative project solution. Other steps, such as testing and feedback, will be necessary to see the product or project solution put into action or production.

Designers have long known that the basic design process provides a path to solutions to a wide variety of problems. Businesses have been slow to realize that the essential concepts used by designers can be applied to many more problems than the layout of office cubicles, graphic design of packaging, or the simple aesthetics of an electronic device.

Does all this sound somewhat familiar? To some degree, doesn't it sound like the design process interior designers and architects use to solve design projects? There are plenty of innovative interior designers and architects. There are also many others who come up with the same (or similar) solutions for multiple clients. To a design thinker, this is just like corporations that design "new" products by taking last year's winner and making cosmetic changes. Interior designers must challenge themselves to be more innovative and "design think" to better solve client problems. Since the process is similar, designers in the built environment industry should easily look to thinking outside the box more often.

Of course, there is much more to design thinking than the brief comments provided in this section. Interior designers interested in additional detail about design thinking will find several suggestions in the references.

Design Thinking Lessons for Interior Designers

- Keep designing and seek creative solutions that solve client problems.
- When you can, be innovative in designs for clients; don't "settle" for your first or favorite solution.
- Be particularly innovative in how you organize and manage your practice. Look for ways to do the mundane more elegantly, quickly, and effectively.
- Find ways to better serve clients.
- Collaborate with clients—don't design from only your ego.
- Understand how the users of the spaces they design are actually used in order to have more functional space plans and aesthetic solutions.

CONCLUSION

Problem solving can be argued to be the core task of the designer. Clients have hired the designer to help them with the problem. The design process helps the designer move through the complex process of solving a design problem in an organized fashion. The designer uses skills and knowledge to make decisions that provide the client a solution that meets the client's needs.

In the professional world, problem solving and critical thinking require you to look beyond your own design prejudices or favorite ways of designing to solve the problem presented by the client. Problem solving and critical thinking in a design program help the student learn the processes of design to prepare him or her for the challenges to be faced in the profession.

Interior design in the real world is not the no-holds-barred approach that often is allowed in studio assignments. It is not done in isolation or only for our own gratification. Simple, quick answers that have no relationship to the needs and wants of the client are rarely appropriate. A thoughtful approach to finding the best answer is important—not only in the academic setting but in the real world as well. Reality costs money.

FOR DISCUSSION

These discussion items and scenario cases require you to use critical thinking to solve one or more problems. In many of these items and cases, you must take the role of a design practice business owner or a practicing designer. There is no *one* right answer to any of these discussion items or scenarios.

1. A client wants a new sofa for his living room. What must you find out from the client in order to properly specify a sofa?

2. A client has asked you to design a residence. Discuss during which phase of a project each of these tasks would take place:
   - Selecting sustainable flooring materials
   - Evaluating the floor plan against fire safety issues
   - Determining which fee method to use

3. You are very passionate about sustainable design practice and the use of sustainable products. Should you specify sustainable materials for a project when the client has already expressed no interest in using those kinds of items?

4. The client has told you she likes the colors green and orange for her pediatrics office. What do you need to know to clarify her color preferences so you can make recommendations?

5. Create a to-do list of what you must do one day this week. Prioritize that list, with the most important items noted first. Also note any items that could be put off until the next day. Prepare a brief sentence justifying your decisions as to what tasks must be done first versus those that can be put off.

6. How can the design thinking philosophy change the way interior designers approach a project, such as a residence, a commercial office space, or a school?

Cases for Discussion

1. "When we did a bathroom remodel years ago, we initially hired a designer to draw up plans for us. This gentleman came with good credentials—years of experience, teaching classes at a university, and so on. Well, he was definitely creative, but he overwhelmed us with this initial assortment of plans—many of which were way off the wall—especially for a conservative couple. Some ideas were not even 'doable,' such as putting a glass-enclosed shower outside on the deck—huh? It was like he was purposefully just trying to impress us with the multitude of ideas he could come up with. When we asked for something more modest, he acted as though it were an insult to his creativity. He did come back with some more traditional plans but with extravagant prices for all the fixtures, cabinetry, and the like. He again acted offended when we requested to see some possible alternatives that would not be quite so expensive. We finally decided to not go with any of his ideas, paid him his fee, and were relieved to see him go. Yes, he was creative, but he did not seem to approach the project critically—just bouncing from one idea to another. We soon lost confidence. If he had come to us with one or two carefully thought out and organized plans and the willingness to consider our specific needs structurally and financially, we would

have been much more impressed." (Story provided by Barbara Robbins)

■ How could the designer have handled the second meeting so that a more positive result for himself and the client occur?

■ What do you see as the issue the designer needs to address about how he approaches his work with the client?

2. Mr. Jones has contacted you to help him resolve issues and necessary changes to his house now that his wife is in a wheelchair. The house was not built for wheelchair clearances. It is a standard single-story, 1,800-square-foot tract house with three bedrooms—including one master bedroom—and two baths. The master bath has a tub/shower. There is a small kitchen that is open on the stove side to the family room.

■ Determine what the overriding problem is to help Mr. Jones with this potential project.

■ List five questions you would want to ask or information items you must gather in order to decide how to proceed with this project.

3. Diane agreed to participate in a project for a charitable foundation's new office. She was contacted and teamed with Sally, a designer from another firm who is on the board of the charity. The foundation has very little money to purchase furnishings. Sally, using her contacts, has already secured donations for the paint and new carpeting. They want to complete the project in six weeks for the anniversary of the charity's opening.

Diane took on this project (for no fee) because of her interest in the charity and Sally's involvement. Sally also promised Diane that a staff member from Sally's office would be available to help. Two weeks into the project, Sally made excuses for herself and her staff member and dropped everything into

Diane's hands. Sally had previously given Diane some notes from a board meeting that indicated how the board wanted the offices to be designed. Diane had obtained the floor plans from the charity's office staff, but it was obvious to Diane that the space needed to be site measured.

- Define the problem or problems that exist for Diane.

- Develop solutions to get the project moving.

- Determine what must be done to get the project completed.

NOTES

1. Linda Tischler, "IDEO's David Kelley on 'Design Thinking,'" www .fastcompany.com, January 14, 2009, p. 4.
2. Tim Brown, "Design Thinking," *Harvard Business Review*, June 2008: 86.
3. Tim Brown, *Change by Design* (New York: HarperCollins, 2009), 16.

3

Problem Definition and Analysis

As you no doubt know by now, interior design projects are more than making selections of furniture and fabrics. Design projects are, for the most part, complex undertakings that require much thought. Each is also different even when they are "similar," such as when one designer is responsible for the design of multiple residences. Thus each is a design problem in itself. Consider each of the following:

- Design a dental office using open office furniture instead of casework.
- Remodel a 2,500-square-foot house to accommodate an extended family of eight.
- Convert a three-story residence in a historic district to a bed and breakfast.

Each is a design project that will test the interior designer's skills and knowledge. They can easily be restrained by client budget limits and even internal firm challenges. Understanding the problem presented by the project is critical, as it impacts the work of the design firm, individual designers assigned to the project, and the firm itself.

Interior design is not just the expression of creativity and development of aesthetic results that bring many into the profession. The interior designer must solve the problem. Regardless of the type of project, the financial situation of the client, and the experience of the designer, problem solving is the engine of the profession. What takes place throughout the process is the accomplishment of tasks and applications of knowledge to solve problems. Creativity and aesthetics—although very important—are only part of the included tasks.

Problem solving design solutions also involves the ability to think critically. Some project problems might have multiple options that could work. The designer must use critical thinking in order to determine which option is the best solution for the client's situation and needs. There is always more than one way to prepare a floor plan for an office—or any other type of facility. There are numerous ways to develop a color scheme or fabrics to choose for, say, seating in a physician's suite. It is the designer's responsibility to think through each task and offer the client the best solution in the best interests of the client. It starts with clearly defining the problem.

GOALS AND OBJECTIVES

You no doubt have learned how setting goals and objectives is important in the achievement of personal and professional success. Design projects also involve setting goals and objectives. Having clearly defined project goals and objectives helps you or your design team in its work by creating direction. A project needs a "road map" in order to improve the overall success of a design project for the client and the designer. According to Peña and Parshall, "Project goals indicate what the client wants to achieve, and why."[1]

Setting goals and objectives is also important for businesses to help them achieve success. A design business taking one day at a time without thoughtful goals leads to business failure more commonly than business success. Certainly, it takes time to establish goals and objectives, but it is time well spent.

Since a number of books make little distinction between a goal and an objective, it is important to clarify what each term means in our context for this book. A *goal* is something that a person, company, or client wishes to achieve. It might be considered the end point. They are commonly broad statements and can take many forms, depending on who is establishing the goal and the purposes behind setting the goal. A goal for a gift store, for example, might be to increase the store's revenue through a new design.

Since each goal can be rather complex, it is necessary to plan in detail how to accomplish the goal. Thus, objectives are also required to help achieve the goals. *Objectives*, when considered separately from the meaning of goal, are actions or tasks that, if accomplished, help achieve the goals in a more organized fashion. Objectives are stated in more detail and often include a timeline for accomplishment. An example of an objective for the gift store is to remodel the store to increase the flow of customers through the store.

Project Goals and Objectives

Project goals are specific ends that the design team and client wish to achieve. According to Kilmer and Kilmer, "The goals of a project state what the client wants to accomplish and why; they involve trying to ascertain the client's values and needs, including physical, social, economic, and psychological."[2] Commercial projects may also have business goals that impact the project design goals. Obviously, the more complex the project, the more important becomes goal and objective development.

The client may have a goal to achieve a design of a restaurant that will bring in a hip, young crowd. Although only one goal was stated, the designer is likely to learn through programming questions that the project has many goals. It would not be improbable that some of those goals will be in conflict with one another. For example, another goal for this restaurant might be to create a Leadership in Energy and Environmental Design (LEED®) certified project. The owner may wish to do this for a number of reasons. This second goal may be in conflict with another issue—that is, the owner has limited funding for the design and FF&E. Finding a way to achieve all the project goals will be part of the challenge for the designer.

Of course, the designer hired for the restaurant project may have her own goals for doing this project. Perhaps the designer wishes to enter the project in a design competition. The design firm might naturally have a goal to make a profit on the execution of the design of the restaurant. As can be seen, goals for a project can take many forms for the stakeholders involved.

An Example of Project Goals
Provided by: Suzan Globus, FASID, LEED AP, NJCID, Globus Design Associates. Fair Haven, NJ

Some Background Information
This suburban New Jersey public library is located across the street from a middle school and is a popular after-school destination for the teenage students. Their behavior had become increasingly

unruly, to the point where the staff felt menaced and called the police, resulting in a student's being handcuffed and arrested. After futile attempts to negotiate with the town government for increased police presence during after-school hours, the library board voted to close the library after school. After national media coverage and negotiations with the mayor, the library board reopened the library during after-school hours.

Project Goals and Objectives

To redesign the young adults' area of the library to encourage appropriate behavior.

Client Goals (client defined as library board): To encourage quiet study, provide space and resources for homework, and increase opportunities to develop a love for reading; to segregate the young adult space from the rest of the library to reduce the complaints about noise from the adult library patrons.

Client Goals (client defined as library staff): To improve sight lines and security; to provide space for small groups to study or socialize; to provide space for small-group computer instruction, gaming, and other library program activities, as well as individual quiet study space.

Client Goals (client defined as teens who use library): To increase the number of computers so teens don't have to wait to use them; to provide small-group spaces to work on projects or socialize; to separate quiet study areas and to provide help with resources; to be able to drink and eat snacks in the library.

Designer's Goals: To address all of the three groups' goals in the design solution within the budget and time allotted; to create ownership of outcomes among the client groups during the process.

Project Issues: To gain a consensus regarding the project goals; to assist the library board to broaden their definition of reading to

(continued)

include more than books and definition of appropriate behavior for teens; to provide evidence that technology can be used to create community among young adults instead of alienating them, as many board members felt; to reduce noise in an open space without reducing sight lines.

Concept Statements: To create an inspiring environment for the teens that supports scholarship, community, and appropriate behavior; to design a young adults area that will become a source of pride for the library board, staff, and community at large.

Now let's look at objectives. Any one goal could reasonably have multiple objectives. Careful planning of objectives helps the design have a better chance of achieving the goal. This is because the "how" (objectives) is figured out along with the "what" (the goal). Since they are more detailed and task oriented, objectives are often easier to prepare. For example, for the client, the goal of hiring a design firm that is known for cutting-edge design can include several objectives: research local and out-of-state design firms known for hospitality design on the Internet, prepare some sort of *request for proposal (RFP)* document to send out to various firms, set up the appointment meeting for the firms responding to the RFP, and so forth.

An objective for the designer wishing to respond to the **RFP** for the restaurant might be to research the likes and dislikes of generations X and Y to establish what restaurants they like. This research will help the designer create an exciting interior that will attract that young, hip customer. A business objective for the design firm could be to insist on careful time record keeping and other project management techniques to keep the project on budget.

Business Goals and Objectives

Business goals are ends that a business wishes to achieve. A business can establish numerous business goals concerning marketing, revenue, staff, financial performance, and other areas of the business. A common business goal is to increase revenue or profit.

A very formal way of establishing long-range business goals and objectives is through a process called *strategic planning*. "Strategic planning is a process for creating a specific written vision for the design firm and its future."* Less formal business planning is simply called *annual planning*. Strategic planning is most often done to plan three or more years into the future, while an annual plan is obviously prepared for the coming year.

During strategic planning, a technique called *SWOT analysis* is used. SWOT stands for strengths, weaknesses, opportunities, and threats. Strengths and weaknesses are related to internal factors, such as the reputation and experiences of the firm or designer. An example of a strength might be the number of years a firm has been in business. A weakness might be the lack of experience a designer has in a particular specialty. Opportunities and threats are related to external factors or those that are outside the firm. An example of an opportunity might be a report that a major business has decided to move 3,000 employees into the market of a design firm. Threats can be potentially damaging to the firm. An example of a damaging threat was played out during the recession. The collapse of

---

*Christine M. Piotrowski, *Professional Practice for Interior Designers*, 4th ed. (Hoboken, NJ: John Wiley & Sons, 2008), 203.

(continued)

the mortgage market stopped large numbers of people from building or buying new homes.

The purpose of doing long-range strategic planning is to allow the firm to look into the future and anticipate change. Certainly, the sole practitioner may be most concerned with what is going on in the present. However, any size business can benefit from looking at least two to three years into the future. It can help the firm budget for new computers that might be needed, or to hire additional staff. Strategic planning forces the firm to be future oriented so that the owner and staff will stretch themselves—but with thought.

Another type of planning that benefits a design firm is annual planning. Goal setting and SWOT analysis can also be utilized to do an annual plan. Obviously, the annual plan is undertaken for essentially the coming year. Of course, some items in the annual plan might carry over to the following year, just as some items in the long-range strategic plan might be items that need to be addressed for only one year.

Strategic reviews of plans on an annual basis allow the firm to keep it current, especially in the face of opportunities or threats. What works well for annual planning is to look at quarterly goals rather than just a year in advance. That makes the process more workable, akin to time management, where large jobs are broken down into smaller "bites."

PROBLEM DEFINITION

Problem solving logically begins by stating the problem. Some refer to this as the *problem definition*. As Peña said, "You can't solve a problem unless you know what it is."[3] A problem definition is a sentence or two that attempts to clarify the problem. An example of a problem definition stated as a question in a design context might be: is there a design flaw in the space plan of the display cases in a gift store that results in customers not walking very far into the store? This definition will help the designer work through programming as well as the beginning design tasks.

Naturally, problem definitions are not limited to interior design projects. Business owners are faced with many problem-solving situations for the business. An example of a problem definition in a business situation is: the design practice is suffering productivity issues since too much compensatory time is taken by staff to make up for overtime.

Problem definitions are sometimes thought of as *design concept statements*. A design concept statement is more detailed than the initial problem definition. The two shouldn't be confused. The design concept statement will be discussed in detail later in the chapter. The "Example of Project Problem Definitions" item provides an illustration of a way to prepare problem definitions.

An Example of Project Problem Definitions

Provided by: Lisa Whited, IIDA, ASID, Whited Planning + Design, Portland, ME

Initial Findings
- Higher levels of stress and depression in medical students compared with age-matched peers.
- Sleep patterns require darkness during day.
- Higher levels of alcohol use in medical students compared with age-matched peers.
- Rate of turnover requires durable, easy-to-maintain finishes and materials.
- Stress alleviated by appropriate organization, design that supports necessary work, and opportunities for socialization.

(continued)

Recommendations

- Well-organized and efficient space.
- Easily moveable furniture in living spaces—ability to control own environment.
- Provide multipurpose furniture that is easily adaptable to specific needs (work, eat, socialize).
- Built-in furniture and shelves in bedrooms to maximize storage (like a yacht).
- Durable, cleanable furniture and finishes.
- Cool, soothing colors and tones.
- In-suite waste separation/recycling.

PROBLEM ANALYSIS

Even the simplest projects or assignments in interior design are complex undertakings. Let us say that the client wants you to "simply" select a new sofa for the living room. Here are just a few of the things you need to consider in this "simple" assignment:

- Assess the existing furniture items to establish a style.
- Determine various client preferences—including price.
- Assess the existing color scheme of the living room.
- Search catalogs or showrooms for appropriate items.
- Discuss pricing and delivery timing with the vendor.
- Obtain agreement from the client on the recommendations.

Your work as an interior designer involves defining and analyzing the problem regardless of its scope. Complex projects naturally involve a greater list of tasks. Your design work also involves solving the problem by determining a course of action to complete the project. In design problem solving, these two critical activities are called *analysis* and *synthesis*.

According to the dictionary, *analysis* is the "detailed examination of the elements or structure of something, typically as a basis for discussion or interpretation. The process of separating some-thing into its constituent elements."[4] Analysis is often contrasted with the term *synthesis*. The dictionary defines synthesis as the "composition or combination of parts or elements so as to form a whole."[5]

Analysis is a predesign and programming task, as was discussed in Chapter 2. It utilizes the information obtained during the earli-est portions of programming to begin to develop ideas on how to solve the design problem. The greater the depth of the informa-tion obtained during programming, the better the analysis will be, thus the greater the opportunity for the success of the project.

Of course, you do not literally jump from the information gathered during programming to drawing floor plans. You use graphic and written tools to help you verify design concepts be-fore moving on to creation of floor plans. *Relationship diagrams* (Figure 3.1), *criteria matrixes* (Figure 3.2), and various kinds of

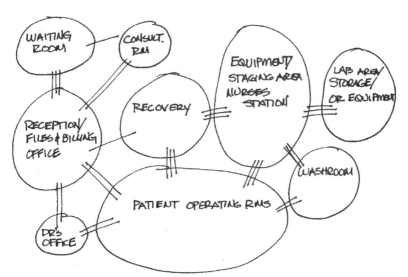

FIGURE 3.1 Relationship diagram. The multiple lines between the "bubbles" indicate the strength or importance of the relationships between jobs or space locations.
Provided by: Laurie Smith, ASID, Piconke Smith Design, Woodridge, IL.

CRITERIA MATRIX FOR: UNIVERSITY CAREER COUNSELING CENTER

	SQ FOOTAGE NEEDS	ADJACENCIES	PUBLIC ACCESS	DAYLIGHT AND/OR VIEW	PRIVACY	PLUMBING	SPECIAL EQUIPMENT	SPECIAL CONSIDERATIONS
① RECEPTION		②⑤	H	Y	N	N	N		TRAFFIC HUB ADJ. TO MAIN ENTRANCE
② INTERVIEW STA.⁽⁴⁾		①④	M	I	L	N	N		FEEL LIKE A TEAM OF FOUR
③ DIRECTOR		④	M	Y	H	N	N		HIGHEST IMAGE ACCESS TO REAR DR FOR PRIVATE EXIT
④ STAFF		③	M	Y	M	N	N		
⑤ SEMINAR RM		①⑥⑦	H	I	H	N	Y		A/V USE IMPORTANT CLOSE TO ENTRANCE
⑥ REST ROOM (2)		CENTRAL	M	N	H	Y	N		
⑦ WORK AREA		②④ CENTRAL	L	N	M	Y	Y		
⑧ COFFEE STATION		CENTRAL	H	Y	N	Y	Y		CONVENIENT FOR EVERYONE
⑨ GUEST APARTMENT		REMOTE	L	Y	H	Y	N		RESIDENTIAL CHARACTER

LEGEND
H = HIGH
M = MEDIUM
L = LOW
Y = YES
N = NO/NONE
I = IMPORTANT BUT NOT REQUIRED

NOTE: IN "ADJACENCIES" COLUMN ⊗ = INDICATES ADJACENCY IMPORTANCE, ⊗ = INDICATES MAJOR ADJACENCY IMPORTANCE

FIGURE 3.2 Criteria matrix.

Provided by: Mark Karlen, Space Planning Basics, 2nd ed. (Hoboken, NJ: John Wiley & Sons, 2004), 17.

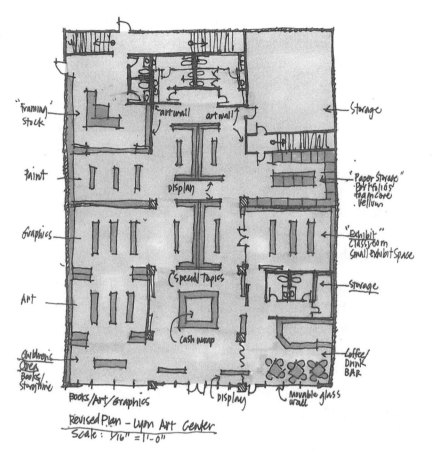

FIGURE 3.3 Concept sketch. The rough layout helps the designer explain to the client the arrangement of spaces and furniture items in each space.
Provided by: Sybil Jane Barrido, ASID, CID, SJvD Design, Long Beach, CA.

quick sketches, such as the one shown in Figure 3.3, are typical tools to help with design analysis. Tools such as programming questionnaires or forms (see Chapter 4) are also used in the analysis.

Analysis also helps you create the criteria you will use to evaluate whether the solutions you offer will really work. Some authors refer to this as *performance requirements*. Peña writes that performance requirements are "those requirements stemming from the unique user needs in terms of the physical, social, and psychological environment to be provided."[6] For the problem definition concerning the store, evaluation criteria might include an analysis of the existing plan to review traffic paths and location of cash register. Even the display of merchandise and the types of fixtures used for the display (criteria that must be collaborated by designer and store owner) must be considered. As the original problem definition stated, customers generally don't move very far into the store but only look at items at the front counters. The floor plan must create a flow of traffic and merchandise display that pulls the customer farther into the store.

It is important to look at the problem definition again after the analysis to be sure that the problem as stated is valid. Sometimes what initially appeared to be the problem is not the primary issue. Analysis can uncover additional problems that are more critical or certainly have a higher degree of priority. For the store, analysis of programming information might discover that fixtures' locations and arrangements impede traffic flow.

SYNTHESIS

As defined above, *synthesis* deals with combining parts into a whole. When someone synthesizes a topic (or design), the individual is bringing together more than one element to arrive at the end or result. It is an important part of solving a problem. Synthesis, as applied to a design project, is considered to be the various steps in the design process where the actual design of a project occurs and the steps are brought together, resulting in an executed project. Of course, synthesis is also used to prepare business and research documents.

In a design project, synthesis involves a whole range of tasks, gradually leading to the solution or solutions that are presented to the client (see Chapter 2). The first step is the use of bubble diagrams. A *bubble diagram* is a two-dimensional drawing that helps the designer visualize such things as location relationships of rooms or areas, communication relationships of groups or individuals, and traffic patterns. Bubble diagrams help the designer with the analysis of the information in order to quickly try out possible solutions (see Figure 3.4).

There are several other types of drawings and documents included in the tasks that make up the synthesis part of the design project. Examples include space plans, furniture floor

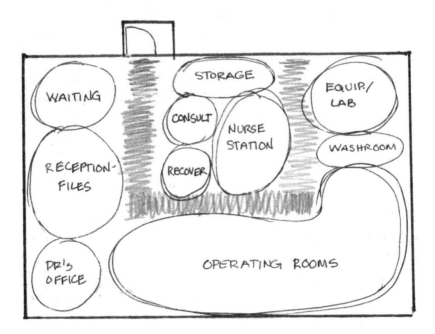

FIGURE 3.4 This bubble diagram corresponds to the relationship diagram in Figure 3.1. Note the changes.
Provided by: Laurie Smith, ASID, Piconke Smith Design, Woodridge, IL.

plans, perspectives, and sketches of details; specification documents indicating what product is to be used where; finalization of equipment and plans produced during the design development stage of the project; and, as the project progresses, documents that result in the construction documents for construction and installation. All these documents and progressively critical problem-solving solutions represent bringing together the information obtained during programming into finalized project documents.

Synthesis also occurs when the designer prepares a written report. In writing a report or a paper, the information reported interprets the information related to the topic in question. An example that all readers can relate to is a paper prepared for a class. For a paper, a topic is chosen, several references are obtained, these sources are analyzed to see how the information relates to the topic, and the information is then interpreted in a logical way. As is necessary, direct quotes that are cited are also normally incorporated. A summary is also included. Professional designers do not write papers in the same way a student does, at least not very often. But they do prepare written reports of various kinds to submit to clients, other stakeholders, and even the boss.

Thus, synthesis thinking and action is what the designer does related to both design projects and written reports. Design solutions are complex arrangements of space, design elements, products, and aesthetics to arrive at the whole—a completed project. Synthesis is a dynamic example of critical thinking. The information that is gathered and analyzed is combined and assessed into possible solutions that solve the project problem and goals.

Integrated Design

Teamwork. You see it when you watch a baseball or football game—individuals with specialized skills and tasks to perform working together to achieve a victory. *Integrated design* recognizes that in the design-build industry the most successful projects bring all the stakeholders together from the beginning of design conceptualization through completion of the project—the victory.

Recent literature has emphasized integrated design practice. It leads to better projects and more satisfied clients. For the most part, the integrated practice models discussed in publications and on the Internet concern situations that bring the architect, engineers, construction managers, and contractors together to work for the client as one group. Those interior designers who work within the large architectural practices are frequently included in the integrated design practice team, but sorely missed being mentioned.

Traditionally, projects progress from the architect to possibly an engineer, then to contractors and subcontractors, with the interior designer perhaps brought in after the building is under construction. The purpose of integrated design is to bring all the stakeholders together for a more cohesive and collaborative design team. The collaborative team is then able to identify project goals more precisely and take advantage of better solutions to complementary issues.

Building a building is a complex undertaking whether it is a single-family residence or a multistory-multiuse facility. Obviously, the bigger the facility, the more complex the problems

(continued)

and the reason integrated design is discussed most often for large complex projects. Clients are pleased when the project runs smoothly, and naturally distressed when coordination between independent stakeholder companies causes delays, cost overruns, and project failures.

Designers need to understand how integrated design practice for projects is a positive—even when the project is a remodeling of a kitchen—not just when it is complex, such as a hotel. Others in the built environment industry need to recognize the important role the interior designer—like every other member of the team—plays in an integrated design project.

A great deal of information can be found on the Internet on this topic. A few items have been included in the references to help you broaden your understanding of integrated design and integrated design practice.

DESIGN CONCEPT STATEMENTS

The term *concept* can be defined as "the underlying or generating thought, idea, philosophy, method, or process for a design proposal or scheme."[7] *Design concepts* are the ideas generated to achieve solutions to the design problem goals. For the design project, they are often expressed in graphic form, generally as sketches and bubbles. A design concept begins to explain how you are going to design the project. It is part of the programming portion of the project process.

The design concept statement is a document in written form that accompanies any graphic design concepts. It should be thought of as a critical document that is created for every project. A *design concept statement* is a "comprehensive verbal perspective of the problem that will precede the detailed program data. This statement should deal with the spirit of the problem, not its details, and represent the broad human, social, aesthetic, and philosophic aspects of the programmer's thoughts concerning the project."[8] It is written before any serious design tasks are begun, not after the project is completed. Review the sample "Design Concept and Concept Statement" to help you understand these design tools.

Design Concept and Concept Statement

Provided by: Robert Wright, FASID, Bast/Wright Interiors, San Diego, CA.

Design Concept

This 2,900-square-foot home in La Jolla was in need of a major remodel from both functional and aesthetic considerations.

THE CLIENT'S PRIMARY GOALS INCLUDE:

- Develop a new open-space plan that takes full advantage of ocean views.
- An enlarged kitchen, spacious dining, and a casual family seating area with television.
- Complete remodel of the kitchen and bathrooms.
- Reconfigure the master suite for more closet space, a lounge area, and an updated bathroom.
- A home office.
- Unify interior and exterior living spaces and use of materials.
- New fireplace design.

THE INTERIOR DESIGNERS ARE RESPONSIBLE FOR ALL ASPECTS OF THE INTERIOR DESIGN, INCLUDING:

- Providing space plan options and the final solution.
- The design and detail drawings for all case goods, built-ins, kitchen and bathroom designs, fireplace, custom doors, and so on.
- The lighting design.
- Design intent drawings including demolition plans, new partition plans, interior elevations and details, lighting plans, telephone/electrical plans, and exterior hard surface plans.

(continued)

- Specifications for kitchen and bathroom fixtures and appliances.
- Interior specifications of all materials and finishes.
- Custom furniture design.
- All furniture specifications and procurement.
- Project administration.

A structural engineer will be contracted to complete the set of drawings.

The space planning and design concepts will be based on the client's ideas to have a home that would be warm and comfortable, family friendly, and flexible for the future. Their additional goals are to someday design the lower, undeveloped level of the home for additional living, entertaining, and guest spaces.

Concept Statement

It has been determined that a clean, modern design would be in keeping with the home's architecture and achieve the client's desires.

A rich blend of materials, including travertine floors throughout the public spaces and the exterior, will help unify the design. Concrete, stone, and wood for the fireplace design will repeat itself in the kitchen as well as in other streamlined built-ins. Walnut veneers mixed with back painted glass and granite counters will be featured in the kitchen. Bifolding retractable doors are to be specified to open the interior living spaces to the inner courtyard as well as the view patio off of the dining area. The master bedroom suite is the one area that the homeowner wants to have a different ambience. It is their retreat, and the design to be developed should be dark and cozy—a great juxtaposition to the open, airy feel of the rest of the house.

The project budget is approximately $200 per square foot, which includes doing work in all areas of the home and some exterior hardscape improvements, window and door replacements and additions, new gates, and upgraded exterior lighting.

The clients are very pleased with the concepts and are excited to get the project going, as they feel that all of their functional needs have been clarified by the designer and the design solutions suggested exceed their expectations.

The design concept statement is often shared with the client to ensure that the designer is interpreting correctly what the client has said. By sharing the design concept statement, the designer will be more at ease that the early design decisions made by the designer are agreeable to the client. Another example of a design concept statement is given in the "An Example of Project Goals" item on pages 38 to 40. Note how the concept statement and problem issues differ.

A Concept Statement and Project Goals

Provided by: Shannon Harris, Member, USGBC, Phoenix, Phoenix, AZ.

Concept Statement: Linking humanity with nature. Cradle is the "alternative" birthplace. The birth center appeals to women and families who believe in natural ways of living. Interiors are composed of natural elements with organic lines. A subtle sophistication in a retreat-like environment creates a safe haven of comfort and relaxation.

Key Project Goals

Aesthetic/Stylistic: Make a connection between modernism and natural elements. A modern look and feel infused with organic elements enhances the patient's decision of natural birth. Nature calms and supports the women for this experience.

Spatial Organization: Separate the birth center from the clinic. Establish strong distinction between the everyday in-and-out appointments of the clinic and the longer hours of stay in the birthing center. Further define the birthing center with residential feel.

Functional/Operational: Provide services for women and their families during and after pregnancy. The clinic will provide for

(continued)

examinations and checkups throughout the nine months, as well as provide spaces for group meetings and educational discussions. The yoga studio will promote healthy exercise for women. The birth center is to include suites for giving birth and large areas of "waiting" for family and friends anticipating the new babies.

Sustainable Goals: Use sustainable practices wherever possible. Mirror city's sustainable practices and support its sustainable efforts.

Mission/Ambience: The space should not feel typical to a medical facility but retreat-like and educational. Overall ambience should be informal and promote open communication between employees and patients. At first sight, clients should feel refreshed and eager to begin their pregnancy.

Unfortunately, there is no standard agreement as to what should be included in a design concept statement. Primary, however, is to explain how the projected design will meet the goals and objectives of the client and the designer. They can be just a few sentences or quite long. A more complex project will naturally require a longer and more detailed concept statement. Some designers and projects create multiple concept statements before beginning schematic design.

A design concept statement usually includes the following items of information:

- The goals and objectives the client has established for a project
- The scope of work
- How you are going to go about meeting the needs and wants of clients and the project
- Outside factors that will influence the design decisions
- Broad description of what the design should express aesthetically and functionally

Design concept statements are useful to any designer for any size project. Clarifying what you are interpreting the client's wishes to be, along with your ideas, at the beginning of the project might seem like extra work, but it actually will save time. Redoing work already accomplished can impact the profits for the firm in doing the project. And while creativity may be the "end result" that many designers imagine for a project, profits keep the firm in operation and staff members working.

Here are some key elements to keep in mind when producing a design concept statement:

- Always keep it as concise as is reasonable.
- Use broad statements that provide direction.
- Explicitly described details are kept to a minimum.
- It contains ideas as to what *will* be done, not simply an explanation of what *was* done.
- It is written before the project is begun.
- It is not carved in stone and can be modified as the project progresses.

CONCLUSION

Design project planning begins with stating the goals and objectives of the project. Once goals are established, the problems related to the goals are specified. Problem solving requires clearly understanding and stating the problem. Sometimes that problem is obvious. Sometimes it is made clear only after analysis of an initial problem statement.

Project problem definitions result from information obtained during the programming phase. Usually, they are simple statements by the client that they want the designer to "do something"—be it select new furniture or design whole facilities.

The questions and information gathered by the designer during the in-depth programming helps the interior designer analyze the problem and determine if there is another problem in addition to the initial one.

For a project, the preparation of a design concept statement helps show the way to the solution. It projects answers to questions as well as describes likely solutions, though those may change. Those changes should be subtle, not dramatic. Dramatic differences between the original design concept statement and the final solution means that the designer misinterpreted many things.

FOR DISCUSSION

These discussion items and scenario cases require you to use critical thinking to solve one or more problems. In many of these items and cases, you must take the role of a design practice business owner or a practicing designer. There is no *one* right answer to any of these discussion items or scenarios.

1. Refer to the "Project Goals and Objectives" section starting on page 37. Reread the example about the restaurant in that section. Prepare a list of three objectives that might also exist but were not stated by the restaurant owner. Discuss why you think these objectives are valid.

2. Using the information from the text and what you prepared for item 1, clarify the design problem.

3. Originally, a dorm room was designed to accommodate only one student. Due to major construction on another dorm building, it is necessary to convert the single rooms to doubles. All the standard functional spaces are required for each student.

- Develop a design problem statement and a design concept statement for the redesign of dorm rooms so they can accommodate two students.

4. Two members of your design staff have been taking a lot of time off—with pay—now that a major project has been completed. It was necessary for these two designers to work numerous hours of extra time in order to get the project completed on schedule. Other staff members are resentful of the missing designers and the additional work they must do in their absence.

- Analyze the business problem(s) that now exist and prepare at least two solutions to prevent this from happening in the future.

5. Explain how a designer can use the graphics discussed in this chapter to help the client visualize a floor plan for a summer cabin. The cabin will have a large living space, a kitchen/eating area, two bedrooms, and a full bath.

6. National Hospital (a fictitious company) hired your firm to help them update the west lobby of the hospital. This lobby is in the oldest part of the hospital, built in the 1950s. It was last updated in the early 1980s. It now serves as a waiting area for patients to be admitted for nonemergency surgery. An incoming patient will wait here until called by an admitting attendant to fill out paperwork. After these forms are completed, the patient and family members are escorted to the second-floor surgery waiting area.

The lobby is drab and somewhat dark, with only a limited amount of natural daylight. The seating consists of individual small armchairs, as are commonly used in physicians' waiting rooms. The hospital desires you to redesign the space to help make patients and family members more at ease. They want a color scheme that is soothing and will be appropriate for the next five years.

■ Prepare a design problem statement and a design concept statement.

Cases for Discussion

1. Your client needs to have his wife's 67-year-old mother move into the house. The mother has begun to show signs of Alzheimer's disease and has other health problems as well. They want you to convert part of the house into a separate living space for the mother.

   The two back bedrooms are connecting and separated by closets. Entry to the bedrooms is currently from a large hall so that each door faces directly into the hall. Each bedroom is 12 feet by 14 feet, not including the closets. The left wall of the bedroom on the left adjoins the master bath. The apartment would require a full bath, bed space, and a small sitting area. The apartment should also be able to accommodate a hospital-type bed if the mother needs more nursing care in the future.

   ■ Prepare a design problem statement and a design concept statement for this client request.

2. Rebecca opened her own design firm eight years ago after working three years for a residential furniture showroom and design firm. Those contacts allowed her to focus on high-end residential clients in her state. Her business grew slowly but positively, with sufficient revenues and work to necessitate hiring an office assistant after four years. At that same time, she moved from her home office to a small commercial office space in a shopping center located in the vicinity of the high-end clients she was targeting.

Her practice continued to grow regarding the quality of projects, having connected with two custom builders. Rebecca decided in late 2006 to add another assistant. It meant moving to another office space to comfortably hold the staff and resource library. She wanted to stay in the same area and ultimately leased space larger than her office needs. Thus, Rebecca decided to make part of the extra space a small showroom.

The showroom was first filled with some of the return items that Rebecca had taken back from clients over the years. Only the best pieces were displayed. She also added many additional items, especially accessories and small furniture items, such as end tables, and small cabinet items.

The loan for the new display furniture items was obtained based on two projects that one of the builders assured Rebecca would be started in early 2007. One project was started and now (2009) is nearly completed. However, that homeowner has recently defaulted on the construction loan balance. The second project was stopped in 2008 as site work began.

In early 2009, Rebecca laid off the assistant hired in 2006 and cut the other assistant to part time. She is considering laying off the other assistant, but needs some help for the few walk-in customers that still enter the studio/showroom. By using her reserve funds, Rebecca has been able to keep up with her rent and other business expenses, but that will not last much longer.

- Identify any problems that exist regarding her business operations and staff.

- Be prepared to discuss solutions to the problems you have identified.

3. Grant was on a preliminary call with another designer, Thomas. The client was a person Grant knew, so Thomas expected him to take the lead in the meeting. After some preliminaries, Grant seemed to be distracted, and Thomas had to ask the client a number of questions about needs and project goals. On the way back to the office, Thomas asked Grant why he wasn't more engaged with the client. Grant admitted that clients who just didn't seem to "get it" right off the bat turned Grant off and thus Grant "tuned them out." Grant wasn't sure why he did it other than he assumed the client was just a poor client. Thomas said he thought the problem was something else because the client responded well to Thomas and was enthusiastic to get started.

- What are the problems (if any) that appear to exist between Thomas and Grant?

- Assume that Grant is the senior designer, but not owner of the design firm. What actions, if any, should Thomas take?

NOTES

1. William M. Peña and Steven A. Parshall, *Problem Seeking*, 4th ed. (Hoboken, NJ: John Wiley & Sons, 2001), 68.
2. Rosemary Kilmer and W. Otie Kilmer, *Designing Interiors* (Fort Worth, TX: Harcourt Brace Jovanovich, 1992), 181.
3. Peña and Parshall, p. 15.
4. *The Oxford American College Dictionary* (New York: Oxford University Press, 2002), 41.
5. Philip Babcock Grove, ed. *Webster's Third New International Dictionary* (Springfield, MA: Merriam-Webster, 1993), 2321.
6. Peña and Parshall, p. 110.
7. Nikolas Davies and Erkki Jokiniemi, *Dictionary of Architecture & Building Construction* (Burlington, MA: Architectural Press/Elsevier, 2008), 89.
8. Mark Karlen, *Space Planning Basics*, 2nd ed. (Hoboken, NJ: John Wiley & Sons, 2004), 7.

4

Asking Questions

Nobody knows everything about everything—although some seem to think they do. We learn a lot about what we don't know by asking questions. We use questions throughout the design project process to gain information. We use questions in order to effectively operate the business. We also use questions to think critically and make all manner of decisions. Business schools (as well as other programs) use questions to help students learn or even "teach themselves." Referred to as the *Socratic method,* it is "a method of teaching that explores topics or seeks to enhance understanding through question-asking and dialogue, rather than didactic presentations."[1] It is often thought of as a cornerstone of critical thinking.

Students and entry-level designers at times are afraid to ask questions. They don't want to look like they don't know. In reality, maybe it is because they do not feel comfortable in knowing what questions to ask. Lacking in experience, designers who are new to practice don't know what to ask or how to ask for information from a client, a coworker, or the owner.

Never fear, as even the most experienced professional designer must ask questions. The experienced professional may have designed 25 or even 250 medical office suites, but he hasn't designed one for the new client with whom he has never worked. For that matter, he hasn't designed the new office suite for a previous client, either, since client needs have likely changed. You have heard it before—"there is no such thing as a dumb question." Perhaps the dumb questions are those that are not asked when information is needed to make a decision.

THE PURPOSE OF ASKING QUESTIONS

Asking questions should always be thought of as a dialogue, not your dominating the conversation in some way. By asking questions, you are searching for information that the other person may be reluctant to openly communicate. Clients don't always know what to tell you or how to tell you what they need concerning the project. Always remember that in asking questions the exchange will be a two-way street, as your questions may spark questions from the client to you.

Questions asked during the programming phase of the project are crucial. Forgetting to ask something as seemingly simple as color preferences can cause extra work and even loss of revenue. However, that is not the only time when questions are asked and might be crucial to the success of the project from both the client's and your point of view.

Designers generally find that they must ask many questions during the presentation of design concepts. These questions are used to help obtain agreement to the concepts (Figure 4.1). If agreement does not initially occur, then questions are needed to find out what the objections are and to work toward understanding and finding a new solution.

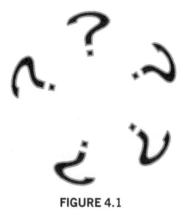

FIGURE 4.1

Here are examples of a few other situations that require designers to ask questions beyond those needed to complete a project:

- Business operations and management questions, such as those related to hiring staff.
- The designer will have questions about client payments.
- Questions to clarify who the decision makers are.
- Specific product performance questions to vendors and suppliers.
- Questions concerning how to solve business issues.

Naturally, clients also have many questions. It is their way of finding out specific details and information about the designer and the designer's thinking. The first questions the client will ask concern the designer's credentials and abilities. Others will be about the design process, as many clients will be unfamiliar with how a project is completed. They will also ask many questions about "why" something is done or a particular product is selected. Realize that it is very important to answer questions honestly, without feeling that the client is "interfering." Because of shows on television, magazines, and salespeople clients may have talked to in stores before they hired the designer, they may have a lot of ideas about design that are not necessarily appropriate solutions to their specific problems and needs.

Designers must be careful in using industry *jargon*—words that are essentially industry specific—when talking to clients. Some designers feel that using industry terms makes them sound more "professional," and in some respects it certainly means the designer is knowledgeable. But jargon can also confuse a client or embarrass a client, since he would not want to appear to be uninformed.

Questions also help you think critically. If you don't ask questions, you are accepting information at face value. It can mean that you are assuming the source of the information is 100 percent correct. Asking questions makes you a better learner, a better designer, and a better citizen. Your decision making will improve as you become comfortable with asking the right questions. Never be reluctant to ask a question when something isn't clear.

Questions Help Define Project Criteria

Provided by: Michael A. Thomas, FASID, CAPS, Design Collective Group, Scottsdale, AZ.

Defining project criteria is an absolute and critical step for all design projects, no matter the shape or size of the job. Two very important and essential things flow from that process: the scope of work and the letter of agreement. In fact, the success (or failure) of the entire project and client relationship can almost be predetermined by how well the design team identifies that baseline of information.

So how and when does that process of assembling the project criteria begin? In an American Society of Interior Designers

(ASID) continuing education workshop conducted by Dr. Stuart Rose more than two decades ago, I learned key ways to accomplish that objective. He said that forming that baseline of criteria starts in those few, sometimes awkward moments when designer and client come together for the initial interview.

Dr. Rose explained that designer-client bonds are a key to success of any project or relationship. And in order to form a bond during that first interview, the designer is responsible for creating an atmosphere of trust—a kind of unique understanding not unlike that of a doctor and patient. After all, the goal of that initial appointment with the medical professional is to identify sufficient information so that a diagnosis can be developed and a prescription written that will make the patient better. It's the same for designers. We need qualitative and quantifiable information from the client so that a scope of work can be developed and a proposal for services created for client consideration.

The challenge is that too often designers jump to conclusions about what all is to be provided, offering a contract for client review before they know what all the project requirements of the job will be.

Dr. Rose further suggested that professionals create a trusting atmosphere that will encourage a flow of information, details, and expectations from client to designer. He emphasized that we need to learn not only to listen, but to listen with intent and discipline. Start by asking only broad, open-ended questions, briefly repeating those responses for further clarification and in order to keep the client talking as much as possible.

What I remember most clearly from Dr. Rose's class is his recommendation for that very first interview question. At the

(continued)

beginning of the meeting, he said to ask the potential client, *"How did you come to realize that you needed the services of an interior designer?"* I have used that question repeatedly in meetings with clients and discovered that it puts them at ease. It seems to get them thinking broadly, nearly philosophically, rather than an initial deep dive into details.

If you ask those broad questions before probing for details, a great deal can be revealed about what the client is thinking, what the priorities might be, who else is involved with the project, and even time frames and financial factors. Having as much information as one can glean is critical to the formation of the project criteria and then the agreement. It can also establish a long-term, mutually beneficial relationship between designer and client.

LISTENING SKILLS

An important corollary to asking questions is listening carefully. Active listening is an important skill for a design professional whose job involves interpreting information and solving problems. We are all guilty at times of not listening. Students turn off instructors; designers don't hear what the client has said; designers don't hear what the project manager said; and so on. Part of the reason we don't always hear everything is that we are constantly processing huge amounts of information. Another reason is that one party to the conversation is so intent on what she wants to say next, she doesn't listen to what the other person is saying right now. Then there is always the case of one person who is so involved in talking that she forgets to let the other person talk. Designers are often guilty of rambling on and on during an initial interview about how great a designer they are that they miss important needs and wants of the client.

Few will admit to being a poor listener. If we can hear, we also believe we listen. There is a difference between hearing and listening. Hearing means that you can discern sounds. *Listening* is active and involves attention to the source of the sound. If you are not paying attention, you are not truly listening, even though you can hear the sounds the other person is making. "On average, people are only about 25 percent effective as listeners."[2] That means we are missing a lot of information that people are trying to communicate to us.

Here are several key points to help you understand why listening is crucial to your professional and personal life:

- You learn more by listening than by talking.
- Actively listening to clients (and others) tells them you are really interested in them.
- People respond better to those whom they perceive as really listening to them.
- Listening helps you become a more confident person.
- Listening helps you keep an open mind and enhance your critical thinking skills.
- Good listening is very important in team assignments.

There are all sorts of stories that could be told about the effect of poor listening. This story, told to me by a designer, is a great example: At a meeting with a client and a sales associate from an office furnishings dealer, the designer asked the client about furniture needs and styles and then switched to color preferences. The client responded that he had a preference for tans and greens, saying, "I really don't like blue at all." Almost the next question from the sales associate was, "And what would you think about using blue on the chairs?" You can imagine what the client thought of the sales associate.

You must learn to be a good listener. Listening attentively, asking questions, and listening again helps the client realize you are interested in solving her problems and designing the project for what she needs. It is also a skill that enhances your critical thinking abilities to solve problems not only for the client, but others that impact you personally or otherwise professionally.

Become a better listener by consciously deciding to listen to others rather than worry about what you want to say. Ask a trusted friend to evaluate your listening skills. Have they seen—or experienced—you interrupting others or acting distracted when you talk to them or others? Maybe they have experienced or seen other traits of bad listening. Take their comments as friendly advice to improve you and your confidence.

Changing any bad habit is not easy. Improving your listening skills will serve to make you a more critical thinker and better designer. By being a better listener you will also find people are listening to you more. And this will help you be a better designer and leader. Table 4.1 provides a few tips to improve your listening skills.

TABLE 4.1. Tips for Good Listening

Don't interrupt!
Use eye contact to help you connect with the speaker.
Don't "hijack" the conversation by taking it in another direction.
Ask questions that will help you understand the speaker's comments better—after the speaker has finished.
Mirror back or paraphrase key points so that the speaker knows you have listened.

ASKING QUESTIONS   **71**

ASKING THE RIGHT QUESTIONS

Of course, a big key in asking questions is asking the right questions. The right questions help you learn information needed to complete the project. They help you understand objections when they are raised and help you clarify information when the client appears not to understand your concepts. The right questions help you understand business issues that may be holding back your company. In other words, the right questions help you gain the genuine answers that move the conversation and encounter along to a positive conclusion regardless of the situation.

Asking the right questions is definitely a part of critical thinking. People don't always say what they mean, and sometimes tell the listener what they think they want to hear. A critical thinker has to keep that in mind and realize that more than one question might be needed to get the complete answer.

There is no one "right" and perfect question for every situation. That is why it is important to learn questioning techniques. A "right" question:

- Will help you get the information you need.
- Is easy for the listener to understand.
- Is unlikely to cause distrust or misinterpretation by the listener.

One method to get the information needed via questions is to use the basic question starters used by journalists—Who, What, When, Where, Why, and How. A few other question starters for the designer are "How much" and "What if ..." Here are a few examples:

- "Who will be using the home office?"
- "When do you need to move into the new restaurant space?"

- "Why do you want to replace all the furniture in the living room?"

Of course, there are other ways to pose a question, such as:

- "Do you prefer that patients pay their bills before exiting into the reception room?"
- "Does the family have meals together or informally?"
- "Tell me how you prefer waitstaff to obtain extra condiments, glasses, and silverware."

Types of Questions

Questions can be used to:

- Establish rapport.
- Seek out specific information.
- Create better understanding.
- Clarify general information.
- Encourage a shy respondent to open up.
- Avoid misunderstandings.
- Generate ideas.
- Obtain opinions.

Many designers create check sheets of various kinds to help them remember what to typically ask. This is especially useful during programming. Figure 4.2 is an example of programming questionnaire. These check sheets help even the experienced designer remember to ask important information that could delay the progress of the project.

Miramonte
Kingston Upon Thames

GM.01 Living Room

Main House - Ground Level

Function
- ☐ Entrance
- ☐ Gathering Area
- ☐ First Impression
- ☐ Determines Interior Concept Image
- ☐ Overflow Space When Entertaining
- ☐ Formal Use for Formal Gathering
- ☐ Waiting Area for Driver/Valet
- ☐ Seating Group Quantity
- ☐ Other

Color
- ☐ Jewel Tones
- ☐ Light
- ☐ Monotone
- ☐ Pastel
- ☐ Color Preference
- ☐ Other

Image
- ☐ Formal
- ☐ Traditional
- ☐ Period Preference
- ☐ Eclectic
- ☐ Other

Flooring Material
- ☐ Smooth
- ☐ Stone
- ☐ Honed Finish (no shine natural)
- ☐ Polish Finish
- ☐ Decorative Carpet
- ☐ Wood
- ☐ Other

Voice Data/Telephone Location
- ☐ Near Seating Group
- ☐ Entry for Valet or Service
- ☐ Number of Telephones
- ☐ Other

Special Areas/Focal Point
- ☐ Special Function Requirements (elect.)
- ☐ Fountain
- ☐ Piano
- ☐ Artwork/Sculpture
- ☐ Display Areas
- ☐ Other

Security
- ☐ Interior Monitoring Locations
- ☐ Other

Fabric/Wallcovering
- ☐ Prints
- ☐ Florals
- ☐ Stripes
- ☐ Traditional
- ☐ Formal
- ☐ Other

Existing Furniture/Artwork
- ☐ Identify Quantity
- ☐ Overall Dimensions
- ☐ Preferred Use and Location
- ☐ Other

Background Music System/Controls
- ☐ Location for Control
- ☐ Speakers
- ☐ Others

Metals
- ☐ Brass
- ☐ Chrome
- ☐ Wrought Iron
- ☐ Bronze
- ☐ Other

Lighting
- ☐ Overall Dramatic
- ☐ Recessed
- ☐ Ambient
- ☐ Chandeliers
- ☐ Table Lamps
- ☐ Other

Closet Areas
- ☐ Shoes Sizes
- ☐ Suits ☐ Purses
- ☐ Shirts/Blouses
- ☐ Ties ☐ Hats
- ☐ Long Dresses
- ☐ Misc. Requirements

Drapery Automation
- ☐ Fixed/Open w/ Decorative Treatment
- ☐ Full Function Drapery Treatment
- ☐ Blackout ☐ Other

Materials
- ☐ Marble
- ☐ Decorative Glass
- ☐ Mirror
- ☐ Gold/Gilding
- — Extensive
- — Moderate
- — Minimal
- ☐ Wood
- — Cherry
- — Mahagany
- — Ebony
- — Walnut
- — Exotic
- — Other

Miscellaneous - Special Requirements

FIGURE 4.2 A type of questionnaire used to obtain client and project information during programming.
Provided by: Sybil Jane Barrido, ASID, CID, SJvD Design, Long Beach, CA.

Miramonte
Kingston Upon Thames

GM.02 Study

Main House - Ground Level

Function
- ☐ Entrance
- ☐ Gathering Area
- ☐ First Impression
- ☐ Determines Interior Concept Image
- ☐ Overflow Space When Entertaining
- ☐ Formal Use for Formal Gathering
- ☐ Waiting Area for Driver/Valet
- ☐ Seating Group Quantity
- ☐ Other

Color
- ☐ Jewel Tones
- ☐ Light
- ☐ Monotone
- ☐ Pastel
- ☐ Color Preference
- ☐ Other

Image
- ☐ Formal
- ☐ Traditional
- ☐ Period Preference
- ☐ Eclectic
- ☐ Other

Flooring Material
- ☐ Smooth
- ☐ Stone
- ☐ Honed Finish (no shine natural)
- ☐ Polish Finish
- ☐ Decorative Carpet
- ☐ Wood
- ☐ Other

Voice Data/Telephone Location
- ☐ Near Seating Group
- ☐ Entry for Valet or Service
- ☐ Number of Telephones
- ☐ Other

Special Areas/Focal Point
- ☐ Special Function Requirements (elect.)
- ☐ Fountain
- ☐ Piano
- ☐ Artwork/Sculpture
- ☐ Display Areas
- ☐ Other

Security
- ☐ Interior Monitoring Locations
- ☐ Other

Fabric/Wallcovering
- ☐ Prints
- ☐ Florals
- ☐ Stripes
- ☐ Traditional
- ☐ Formal
- ☐ Other

Existing Furniture/Artwork
- ☐ Identify Quantity
- ☐ Overall Dimensions
- ☐ Preferred Use and Location
- ☐ Other

Background Music System/Controls
- ☐ Location for Control
- ☐ Speakers
- ☐ Others

Metals
- ☐ Brass
- ☐ Chrome
- ☐ Wrought Iron
- ☐ Bronze
- ☐ Other

Lighting
- ☐ Overall Dramatic
- ☐ Recessed
- ☐ Ambient
- ☐ Chandeliers
- ☐ Table Lamps
- ☐ Other

Closet Areas
- ☐ Shoes Sizes
- ☐ Suits ☐ Purses
- ☐ Shirts/Blouses
- ☐ Ties ☐ Hats
- ☐ Long Dresses
- ☐ Misc. Requirements

Drapery Automation
- ☐ Fixed/Open w/ Decorative Treatment
- ☐ Full Function Drapery Treatment
- ☐ Blackout ☐ Other

Miscellaneous - Special Requirements

Materials
- ☐ Marble
- ☐ Decorative Glass
- ☐ Mirror
- ☐ Gold/Gilding
  - — Extensive
  - — Moderate
  - — Minimal
- ☐ Wood
  - — Cherry
  - — Mohagany
  - — Ebony
  - — Walnut
  - — Exotic
  - — Other

FIGURE 4.2 (Continued)

Miramonte
Kingston Upon Thames

GM.03 Dining Room

Function
- ☐ Entrance
- ☐ Gathering Area
- ☐ First Impression
- ☐ Determines Interior Concept Image
- ☐ Overflow Space When Entertaining
- ☐ Formal Use for Formal Gathering
- ☐ Waiting Area for Driver/Valet
- ☐ Seating Group Quantity
- ☐ Other

Color
- ☐ Jewel Tones
- ☐ Light
- ☐ Monotone
- ☐ Pastel
- ☐ Color Preference
- ☐ Other

Image
- ☐ Formal
- ☐ Traditional
- ☐ Period Preference
- ☐ Eclectic
- ☐ Other

Flooring Material
- ☐ Smooth
- ☐ Stone
- ☐ Honed Finish (no shine natural)
- ☐ Polish Finish
- ☐ Decorative Carpet
- ☐ Wood
- ☐ Other

Voice Data/Telephone Location
- ☐ Near Seating Group
- ☐ Entry for Valet or Service
- ☐ Number of Telephones
- ☐ Other

Special Areas/Focal Point
- ☐ Special Function Requirements (elect.)
- ☐ Fountain
- ☐ Piano
- ☐ Artwork/Sculpture
- ☐ Display Areas
- ☐ Other

Security
- ☐ Interior Monitoring Locations
- ☐ Other

Fabric/Wallcovering
- ☐ Prints
- ☐ Florals
- ☐ Stripes
- ☐ Traditional
- ☐ Formal
- ☐ Other

Existing Furniture/Artwork
- ☐ Identify Quantity
- ☐ Overall Dimensions
- ☐ Preferred Use and Location
- ☐ Other

Background Music System/Controls
- ☐ Location for Control
- ☐ Speakers
- ☐ Others

Metals
- ☐ Brass
- ☐ Chrome
- ☐ Wrought Iron
- ☐ Bronze
- ☐ Other

Lighting
- ☐ Overall Dramatic
- ☐ Recessed
- ☐ Ambient
- ☐ Chandeliers
- ☐ Table Lamps
- ☐ Other

Closet Areas
- ☐ Shoes Sizes
- ☐ Suits ☐ Purses
- ☐ Shirts/Blouses
- ☐ Ties ☐ Hats
- ☐ Long Dresses
- ☐ Misc. Requirements

Drapery Automation
- ☐ Fixed/Open w/ Decorative Treatment
- ☐ Full Function Drapery Treatment
- ☐ Blackout ☐ Other

Materials
- ☐ Marble
- ☐ Decorative Glass
- ☐ Mirror
- ☐ Gold/Gilding
- __ Extensive
- __ Moderate
- __ Minimal
- ☐ Wood __ Cherry
- __ Mahogany
- __ Ebony
- __ Walnut
- __ Exotic
- __ Other

Miscellaneous - Special Requirements

FIGURE 4.2 (Continued)

Being tuned in to nuances of *body language* and expression is also important. A person's body language is, according to many experts, often a better indication of what is actually in a person's mind than what is said. There are excellent books concerning body language in the references. Any of these will provide an in-depth discussion of how to interpret body language.

Another part of questioning is realizing that the designer might have the right questions, but that the client (or other party) might not have the answers that the designer really needs. Not all clients know what they want or need. A purchasing agent for a commercial client may have the answers concerning budgets, but not preferences in such things as colors. The designer must be evaluating the answers that the client provides to ensure getting the needed information. Really listening to the answers is critical. It also helps to repeat back what the client is saying before moving on to the next question or any needed response you must provide.

In sales training, salespeople are taught that there are two types of questions. First, there is the *open-ended question*—also called an open probe. It is phrased in such a way that the client will provide an expanded response. For example: "Tell me about your office procedures when a patient comes into the office for an appointment" or "Describe your family's typical use of a family room." When this type of question does not obtain the needed information, you need to use the other type of question, a closed question.

A *closed question*, or closed probe, is used to obtain specific information. Often, the closed question results in a yes or no answer or only one or two words. For the first example, related to the design of the reception/business area, one of the closed types of questions might be "Do you expect patients to pay the copay prior to seeing the doctor?" A closed question related to the second example might be "Does your family eat all meals in the family room?"

In asking questions and thinking critically, some issues bring out strong opinions in many people. Emotional responses are not always fact-filled. Rather than entering into an argument, you might need to ask if it is worth it to continue the discussion. It is important for critical thinkers to know the difference between standing your ground and discussing an issue that might become heated. Thus, you need to ask yourself some questions:

- What is the issue?
- Is the person providing the information biased?
- Is the information vague?
- Is it worth it to continue?

The last one is very interesting, whether the questions are related to general discussions or project questions. We all want to be "right." But sometimes a discussion with some individuals can only lead to anger and bad feelings. Let us say that a designer specified an area rug for a client. The client tells the designer he is sure he saw the same rug on the Internet for $500 less than what the designer is planning to charge. He will not be easily swayed that there are differences that he cannot see. Is this point worth continuing until the client becomes convinced the designer is trying to overcharge him on everything, not just this rug?

Of course, the preceding examples are not the only questions you might ask yourself in thinking critically about many subjects. They will, however, provide a framework for taking into account the information under discussion.

IS THERE ALWAYS A RIGHT ANSWER?

We sometimes want to believe that there always is a "right" answer to any question. To a designer, the right answer helps her get the project moving quickly while allowing her a lot of freedom in creating the project solution. In practice, even when clients think they have the right answer, the designer can offer alternatives. The designer's experience provides these alternatives. Then again, many clients don't always know what they want, but give an answer that must be interpreted by the designer.

It is not that the designer is offering an opposing view to the client's answer. Rather, there are always several options or opinions. Clients, of course, also have reasons for wanting what they believe to be right for them. Questions and the problem-solving process assist the designer in attempting to resolve divergent opinions. Both the designer and client are, after all, on the same "team," with a goal of creating a satisfying project. However, interior designers need to be very careful about allowing their own egos to get in the way of the client's needs. As an interior designer suggested, "Keeping one's ego in check is part of the job as an interior designer."

Similarly, it is important to recognize that, regardless of the topic, there are different opinions or options. Not everyone likes the current trendiest color, belongs to the same political party, believes interior designers should be licensed, or even cheers for the same baseball team to win the World Series. And that is OK. A true critical thinker will understand that not everyone sees the world the way he or she does.

Avoiding Ambiguity

Part of what makes communication difficult is that in the English language, many words have different meanings, sometimes creating *ambiguity* between the parties to a communication. The designer has a particular meaning in mind when communicating with the client (or others) but the listener may not interpret the same meaning. Problems occur when the meanings are confused between speaker and listener. For example, let's look at a few meanings of the word *schedule:*

- Mary needs to complete her schedule for the design director. (A day-to-day plan)
- The project is on schedule. (Indicates a time frame)
- John is scheduled to meet with the client Friday. (An arrangement for something to be done)
- The finish schedule is complete. (A list of paint colors that will be needed in each room)

In interior design, words that "describe" products also can have different meanings. The client may be thinking he needs a desk—an item of furniture with a flat surface and some drawers for storage. The designer knows there are many kinds of "desks" and must be clear as to the need of the client in order to specify the right item. For example, industry-specific terms for desks include executive desk, table desk, operational desk, double-pedestal desk, single-pedestal desk, and systems desk. A desk can also be the counter in a hotel where guests register, a counter at the mall where customers can obtain information, or a counter in a bank where the customer transacts business with the teller.

These simple examples indicate how words need to be chosen carefully to ensure that the meaning the receiver understands is the same as what the speaker meant. It is human nature for most people not to readily admit they do not understand something that is very new to them. Yet it is very possible for clients not to ask when they do not understand. This lack of information can easily lead to errors in the project, rework that must be done, or simply hard feelings between the parties.

BIAS

According to the dictionary, *bias* is "prejudice in favor of or against one thing, person, or group compared with another, usually in a way considered to be unfair."[3] We all have strong feelings about certain issues. An interior designer serving the client must learn to put his or her own bias aside in order to design what is best for the client. At the same time, the interior designer must realize that clients also have bias and might not put their strong feelings aside in order to accept ideas the designer puts forth.

As a critical thinker, it is important to be wary of personal bias as well as biased thinking in others. When two people strongly disagree—and that disagreement is fueled by prejudicial thoughts—effective and positive discussion becomes very difficult, if not impossible. In design, we should be able to put our own bias concerning certain styles of design, products specified, even color schemes aside, in order to serve the client's best interests. Some of these design partialities occur because we have had good luck with certain suppliers or products. It is not particularly a problem to be biased toward a certain supplier if, when it comes time to specify a product for two or three different clients, the decision is made based on client need, not bias. It would be a serious ethical issue if the designer specifies a product because a supplier provides an extra incentive.

It seems that when someone challenges our beliefs, our bias becomes more pronounced. What is more interesting is that most of us don't like to admit to being biased. We all want to be considered fair-minded. It is simply true that all of us have some sort of bias that must be faced. In some situations, that bias can negatively affect the relationship, be it interior designer to client, colleague to colleague, or over many other issues and situations.

AVOIDING DISPUTES

No one begins a relationship with a client, employer, or business associate with the intention of having a dispute. Certainly, not everyone agrees on all topics and certainly not on what is "good" design. Disputes do happen from time to time. The greatest challenge is, of course, to work in such a way as to minimize disputes. When they do occur, it is important to handle them as quickly as possible before one party or another involves an attorney.

Disagreements and disputes can occur on many issues. Disagreements can occur when, for example, the client's understanding of the interior designer's contract conditions is different from the designer's intention. A common example is a dispute that occurs when the client feels that the fabric for a furniture item is different from what the client was expecting. Another example is a dispute over the quality of work done by a tradesperson. Perhaps it is the finish on the floor, or chips in the granite countertop, or the way wallpaper was hung. The designer and the vendor see it one way; the client sees it another.

To resolve a dispute, it is important to consider whether the disagreement is related to factual information or opinions. When the disagreement is concerning facts, one side or the other will need to research the facts or show the evidence to the other party. For example, if the client doesn't understand and objects to design solutions that are building code related, the designer could easily show the client the code language from the appropriate reference.

Changing someone's opinion is much more difficult. We hold opinions closely, sometimes based on years of belief. Someone who has always disliked a certain color will not be easily swayed to use that color in her interior. (My mother always had a pink kitchen and bathroom, so I grew up disliking the color pink!)

Many disputes in interior design are due to the lack of a written agreement before design services begin. The designer understands that he is going to do certain work for the client, while the client feels that the designer will do more than what was done. A written agreement clarifies what will be done before the work actually begins. Written agreements and contracts provide a factual backdrop to help resolve many disputes that occur during a project, since the written agreement provides evidence of the intentions of the two parties.

A common way to handle disputes is through negotiation. *Negotiation* is an activity where we are trying to gain agreement with another party about some issue or issues. Let's say that you and a friend want to go out for dinner but disagree as to where to go. Your friend wants to go to a casual place, and you are interested in something a little "fancy." The give and take that goes on between the two of you to resolve where to eat is negotiation. Should a conflict or dispute arise between the designer and a client or other party, the first effort by the designer will likely be to try to negotiate a resolution. For example, a client feels that the price for a particular product specified for the project is too high. The interior designer may wish to negotiate with the client to resolve the disagreement. The section starting on page 84 on negotiation provides some additional insights into this tactic.

When negotiation does not resolve the dispute, a process called *mediation* may be needed. In mediation, a neutral third party called a *mediator* hears from both sides of the dispute and helps them arrange for a solution. The mediator does not render the decision. The mediator tries to help both sides see the other side's point of view and seek a mutually agreed-upon solution.

The mediator does not force a solution on the two parties in dispute, and suggestions that might come from the mediator are not binding. Figure 4.3 shows you the steps from what is considered to be the most common and least expensive form of dispute resolution to the most complicated and potentially expensive form.

Should mediation also fail to obtain a solution to a dispute, or in very serious disputes that might lead to litigation, a third form of conflict resolution could be in order rather than going to court. *Arbitration,* frequently used in many business situations, is a formal way of resolving a dispute. Once again, a neutral third party, now called an *arbitrator,* will listen to both sides and make a decision. Prior to the arbitration session, both sides have to agree to abide by the decision of the arbitrator. In this sense, an arbitration session is similar to a trial. It is often used in place of litigation so that the parties to the dispute do not have to go to court. Designers regularly include a clause in their contracts and letters of agreement indicating that arbitration would be used to resolve disputes.

FIGURE 4.3 The forms of dispute resolution, from least complicated to most complicated.

NEGOTIATION

As was mentioned earlier, sometimes it is necessary to negotiate a resolution to an issue when both sides feel strongly that they "are right" or want to "win." We have all been in situations where we have proposed something to another person but have had to compromise—at least a little. Maybe it was to get an extra few days to turn in an assignment. It might be to obtain a postponement of an appointment with a client. It could also be discussing a raise with the boss or a pricing discount with a vendor. The back and forth of the discussion with the other party was a form of negotiation.

Often, each side takes a position about the issue and discusses or argues their side. Negotiation is the primary way that disagreements and disputes are settled. Of course, for a negotiation to succeed, each party has to have a willingness to come to an agreement. If one side is adamant about her position, the negotiation will eventually fail.

Win-Win Negotiating

The ideal situation in negotiating is when a conclusion is reached that works for both sides. This is often referred to as *win-win negotiating.* In this situation, both sides are trying to reach agreement to the conflict so that each side is content with the ending arrangement. Win-win negotiating is a discussion by both parties where the dialogue is conducted with both sides behaving and talking ethically and in good faith. Staunchly demanding one's point of view is not win-win negotiating.

In the dialogue with the other party, each side must be willing to listen to the other side's point of view. Of course, each side will have some reasons for their opinions. And some points are always feasibly nonnegotiable. However, to achieve a win-win conclusion, both sides will likely have to bend a little in order for agreement to finally result.

Win-win negotiating requires that you:

- Know your own needs—your own bottom line.
- Are willing to listen and discover what the needs of the client are.
- Be open to the commonalities between parties rather than focusing on the differences.
- Be open to finding solutions that can work for both sides.
- Ideally, create a relationship with the other party rather than looking at the situation as a one-time deal.[4]

Unfortunately, too many "negotiations" are actually one-sided where one party is particularly concerned about winning and has perhaps little concern for the other side's feeling satisfied. This is often thought of as "win-lose" negotiation. Many people think of win-lose negotiations as simply selfish. This type of negotiation occurs when one side holds all the cards. Win-lose negotiations often occur because one of the parties has let his or her ego get in the way of discussing the issue in good faith.

Negotiation Tips

Here are several tips that can help your negotiation sessions be more positive and win-win.

- Plan your negotiation session; don't wing it.
- Cultivate trust between yourself and the other party.
- Be sure you understand who really has the upper hand in the negotiation.

(continued)

- Know what your bottom line is—in other words, when you will walk away.
- Keep your ego in check.
- Not all negotiations will be settled immediately. Some will take multiple sessions.
- Realize that silence can be very powerful. It usually "forces" the other person to talk.
- Seek to achieve a win-win conclusion.

Negotiations will take place throughout the day, not just when you talk to a client. Some will be simple, such as three friends deciding where to go to lunch. Others will be more complex, such as the multiple situations designers will find themselves in when discussing concepts and solutions with clients. Additional information on negotiation strategies can be found in the references.

CONCLUSION

There are innumerable situations in which we must ask questions or questions will be asked of us. Questions bring about understanding regardless of the topic of the question. Of course, questions also can raise emotions if the question challenges beliefs. Questions also can lead to disputes and arguments.

For the designer, questions primarily are used to obtain the information needed from clients and other project stakeholders. How else can the designer find out what the client needs and wants? The designer must challenge herself or himself to develop an attitude and process for positive negotiation and discussion. Positive questioning and negotiation helps everyone to think critically and problem solve projects.

Asking questions develops your critical thinking skills, whether your present situation is as a student or a working professional.

Understanding that your interactions should not be arguments, based on biased opinions or personal ego gratification, helps you be a better professional, business owner, or employee. Thoughtful questions will also enrich your life, as you become a critical thinker ready to engage in meaningful discussions without emotional bias clouding the discussion.

FOR DISCUSSION

These discussion items and scenario cases require you to use critical thinking to solve one or more problems. In many of these items and cases, you must take the role of a design practice business owner or a practicing designer. There is no *one* right answer to any of these discussion items or scenarios.

1. The office manager for a family practice physician has contacted you about potentially remodeling the office suite. The practice has five doctors, three nurses, and an office staff of two besides the office manager. No structural changes are anticipated, but they want a totally new look to the facility.

   - Develop a questionnaire to obtain the information you would need to design this project.

   - Also develop at least three open- and three closed-style questions you would need to ask regarding the project.

2. You need to meet with two manufacturers' representatives in order to decide which product will be appropriate for (a) a high-end residential client who is very particular about the quality of the merchandise to be used in the house, and (b) the owner of a small hotel who wants to replace at least one product in the guest rooms.

   - Decide which of the two choices you will discuss. Be able to describe why you made that choice.

■ Develop at least three to five questions that you feel you must ask the representative in order to determine which of his or her products to specify for the client.

3. Attend a design professional association meeting with a friend. Ask that friend to spend at least one hour observing how you interact with people at the meeting. Have them watch for whether you interrupt, whether you listen attentively, your body language, and other factors mentioned in this chapter. After the meeting, allow them to critique your time at the meeting. What might you need to do to become a better listener? By the way, do the same for the friend at a future meeting.

4. Locate an article or report from a design publication. This should not be an article about a project. After reading the item, describe whether the author showed any lack of clarity, ambiguity, or bias. Do the same for an article on an issue of interest to you, such as the environment, sports, fashion, or any other topic. Apply the same analysis of this article as you applied to the one from the design publication.

5. Designers are frequently faced with negotiating design fees. You have proposed a fee of $10,000 to design a project that will require producing drawings, specifications, and bid documents for a project. The client feels that fee is too high and asks you to lower the fee.

■ If you were in this situation, what would you tell the client as to why your fee is the amount already quoted? What positions must you have ready for your side of the negotiation?

6. Your client can only give you 30 minutes to "make your pitch" and for you ask questions about a proposed project (for a 3,000-square-foot house or a 5,000-square-foot accounting office).

■ What questions would you ask?

■ What points will you make about your competency to complete the project?

Cases for Discussion

1. The owner of a design firm specializing in health care interiors needs to develop a project proposal for a large, independently owned surgical center. The facility will be providing low-risk procedures to outpatients.

   The firm owner assigned part of the design staff the task of developing materials samples for a presentation, while the others used base building drawings to develop sketched floor plans. The turnaround time for this presentation was three days.

   The staff members involved in developing the materials specifications spent many hours looking for two to three possibilities for each item needed (as directed by the owner) and preparing concept groupings of the materials. When the items were shown to the owner, he only selected a piece here and a piece there, meaning that most selections were dismissed and would require additional time for reselection.

   The design team was very frustrated, as they felt that they had come up with very workable materials. In addition to rejecting many of the items (with time running out to make new selections), the owner did not clarify what was wrong with the items rejected or give any additional input as to what he was looking for.

   ■ If you were part of the design staff selecting the materials, how do you believe the whole situation could have been handled so that staff frustration would be at a minimum?

2. As project manager, it is your responsibility along with the design director to assign staff to projects. It was agreed that

Teri and Bill would be responsible for the design of the interior of a golf course clubhouse that was located out of state. The project contract required the design team to visit the site at least twice—during the programming phase and again before installation of architectural finishes. A local design firm was set to supervise the installation of furnishings at the clubhouse.

After their second trip to the site, Bill came to you and said that he thought it would be best to have Teri and himself present for the furniture installation. He said he felt that the other firm's getting involved might diminish the influence of the primary firm and that they would then lose credibility with the client.

- What is the problem here?

- What questions do you need to ask Bill and Teri, as well as the other design firm?

- How would you handle the situation if you indirectly found out that Teri and Bill were dating?

3. Here are three topics in the design/build industry: (a) Frank Lloyd Wright is the greatest architect to influence the interior design profession. (b) It is the designer's responsibility to provide excellent design even when that runs counter to the client's expressed wants and needs. (c) Total commitment to sustainable design is the way the design industry can positively impact the future.

- Choose one of these items that you agree with—even a little. Be prepared to discuss the *opposite point* of view.

NOTES

1. John W. Collins III and Nancy Patricia O'Brien, eds., *The Greenwood Dictionary of Education* (Westport, CN: Greenwood Press, 2003), 330–331.

2. Madelyn Burley-Allen, *Listening: The Forgotten Skill,* 2nd ed. (New York: John Wiley & Sons, 1995), 3.

3. *The Oxford American College Dictionary* (New York: Oxford University Press, 2002), 127.

4. Adapted from Luis R. Gomez-Mejia, David B. Balkin, and Robert L. Cardy, *Management,* 2nd ed. (New York: McGraw-Hill, 2005), 605.

5

Looking for Answers—Research Methodologies

A big part of what an interior designer does with every project is look for answers. Most assume that those answers relate to the questions that occur as a project begins and proceeds. Individuals involved in interior design also look for answers to questions and issues that expand knowledge of the profession. That knowledge "searcher" might be a professional designer, a faculty member, or a student. Research activities to expand one's personal knowledge are certainly personally enriching. Of course, there are those activities that result in an expansion of knowledge for the profession as a whole. Each is of critical importance to the interior design profession.

Research and critical thinking go hand in hand. Many of the issues that you encounter that involve critical thinking will lead you to decide to do more research before you make up your mind. It is a dynamic and important tool in design problem solving and decision making. Let's be clear about what *research* is. Booth, Colomb, and Williams state, "In the broadest terms, we do research whenever we gather information to answer a question that solves a problem."[1] Another definition is: "Research concerns the use of specific strategies and tactics of inquiry to yield new knowledge."[2] The most common arena of research is conducted in the sciences, mathematics, and medicine. Research is also conducted in interior design and architecture.

This chapter is an overview of research methods and processes applicable to the interior design profession. It seeks to provide a general idea to help designers and students understand research and its importance to the profession and the critical thinking component of the training of interior designers.

TYPES OF RESEARCH

Research in interior design can and does go beyond the searches needed to identify the appropriate products to specify for a project. This is, of course, arguably the most common type of research engaged in by the majority of practitioners. Yet additional kinds of research activities are important to the practice of interior design.

One type of research common to the practicing interior designer is *applied research*. In this case, the research "is conducted when a decision must be made about a specific real-life problem."[3] Applied research is used most often in interior design to learn specific information on a topic or situation. Applied research by designers is utilized to help them make better decisions. It is done to carefully investigate the problem rather than make a hasty decision. Returning to a common use of research by designers, perhaps a design firm researches a variety of sustainable flooring materials before making a specification decision. Applied research can also be used to develop design concepts during programming. In some ways, this research is second nature and not even consciously thought of as "research." Another example of applied research would be inventorying existing furniture to determine which items can still be used for the project.

The second type of research is basic or *pure research*. According to Zikmund, this type "attempts to expand the limits of knowledge. It does not directly involve the solution to a particular, pragmatic problem. . . ."[4] Much academic research, such as that conducted by faculty members and graduate students, is considered basic research. Basic or pure research is more formalized and less often conducted by practitioners. Naturally, there are design firms that are interested in creating formalized research, such as firms that prepare evidence-based design research—to be discussed in the next section. In most cases, research of new knowledge by design practitioners occurs for their own use. An example is when a design firm researches last year's clients' satisfaction with design services.

Formal research findings can be obtained from numerous sources. Reviewing formal research is very valuable for any interior designer to help them become more valuable to clients and employers. The following list provides a starting point for locating research findings in interior design:

- The *Journal of Interior Design*, a publication of the Interior Design Educators Council (IDEC)
- The University of Minnesota web site, www.informdesign .umn.edu
- University web sites
- Professional organization web sites
- Books and some trade and professional magazines

Remember that research can also be a business function of the design practice. In business, research is conducted for many reasons. Market research can be performed to determine customer needs for design services. Vendors produce consumer research to find out what consumers want concerning the products they sell. Understanding a design firm's target market (those clients most likely to work with the design firm) is just as important to the overall success of the firm as understanding the needs and wants of individual clients for each project under contract.

EVIDENCE-BASED DESIGN

Design practice keeps changing—as it must—to meet the demands of the profession and clients. Research is an important design skill beyond that needed to find the right products or space-planning solution. Thus, a chapter on research methodologies could not be complete without a brief discussion of *evidence-based design (EBD)*.

But what is evidence-based design? According to Hamilton and Watkins, "Evidence-based design is a process for the conscientious, explicit, and judicious use of current best evidence from research and practice in making critical decisions, together with an informed client, about the design of each individual and unique project."[5]

Evidence-based design seeks to provide documented evidence that designers can use in commercial projects as a basis for design decisions for improved client outcomes. Client *outcomes* or results, by the way, mean different things to different clients. For a hospital it may mean improved infection control; for a business office it might mean improved employee productivity.

Health care projects were the first to incorporate EBD. It is slowly being utilized in support of the design of other types of commercial facilities. The slow application of EBD to other types of commercial facilities is due in part to business owners being concerned with outcomes that are harder to distinguish with research evidence. Although increased employee productivity is a desirable outcome for a corporation, it is not easy to correlate increased productivity to the design of the interior. Thus, the client and designer are less concerned about actually using evidence-based research for other facilities.

Critical Thinking and Evidence-Based Design

Information provided by: Rosalyn Cama, FASID, EDAC. CAMA, Inc., New Haven, CT.

How can interior designers learn critical thought process for their design solutions?

The best way to learn a critical thought process in design is to master the evidence-based design process. Evidence-based design is defined as the process of basing decisions about the built environment on credible research to achieve the best possible outcomes.* Expanded, evidence-based design is an iterative decision-making process that begins with the analysis of current best evidence from an organization as well as from the field; it finds, at the intersection of this knowledge, behavioral, organizational, or economic clues that, when aligned with a stated design objective, can be hypothesized as a beneficial outcome; it does not provide prescriptive solutions, but rather a platform from which to add to an existing base of knowledge or to launch innovation; it espouses an ethical obligation to measure outcomes and share knowledge gained for particular design successes and failures, ideally in a peer-reviewed fashion, as is common in academia.

*Center for Health Design. www.healthdesign.org/edac.

(continued)

> ### *Where can critical thinking advance the profession of interior design?*
>
> If one assumes that an evidence-based design methodology is the way to advance the interior environments we inhabit in order to improve the human condition, then the path toward the innovation of such habitats will be through a critical thought process launched from a baseline of knowledge.

Evidence-based design is not concerned with developing standards that inhibit creative problem solving. On the contrary, it is used to improve unique design. Hamilton and Watkins state, "Used properly, evidence-based design should lead to both more effective outcomes related to design and greater diversity of successful design concepts."[6] The unique nature of every project, proponents argue, allows for new solutions to design problems when EBD is utilized, not cookie-cutter standardized designs.

The EBD research process occurs during the programming or predesign phase, as well as post-construction. At the beginning of a project, information is gathered concerning goals of the project and the different stakeholder needs and wants—similar to most projects. At the end of the project and occupancy, the design is evaluated to determine if goals were achieved and the satisfaction of users of the spaces resulted. Postoccupancy research is particularly important to complete the EBD process. *Postoccupancy evaluation* research is site visits and "project review that are conducted to evaluate the existence of any problems in the design and installation of a project."[7]

This makes EBD sound easy to conduct. It is not. Like all research, it takes time to develop a process for a particular project. It takes expertise in the operations of the business, and it takes time for the designer to develop a research instrument to gather and analyze the data at the conclusion of the study. Careful analysis of information is very important in order to show how the data validates design decisions.

Evidence-based design encourages another positive step in design process philosophy. Designers are finding that collaborative work with the client leads to more effective design. This is counter to the beliefs of many designers who feel the designer knows what is best. This should not be considered an effective way to design in the 21st century.

Knowledge makes the designer more valuable to the client. Certainly, knowledge about design and how to design is important. Nevertheless, knowledge of the client's business is also valuable. Clients tire of teaching designers about their business before the designer tries to proceed with a project. Today, interior designers must thoroughly understand the business of the client in order to be effective. EBD in a sense forces the designer to learn more about the client's business in order to conduct the EBD research.

This chapter cannot provide an in-depth discussion of the process of evidence-based design. There are excellent resources in the references that the reader may wish to review to obtain additional information on EBD.

Postoccupancy Evaluations (POEs)

It is always advisable to know if the client is satisfied with the work the designer has done. Designers learn of success or failure most often from comments the client makes at the time the last of the FF&E is delivered or when the client pays the

(continued)

final bills. Those informal comments are helpful, of course. But sometimes, and for large complex projects, those kinds of informal comments are insufficient to judge the success of a project.

Postoccupancy evaluation is a formal way of obtaining information that helps the designer in the future with similar clients and projects. Some firms refer to this process as the *facility performance evaluation (FPE)*. It is a term that some feel more accurately describes the research process. It is done for the same purposes and is done essentially the same way as a POE. The FPE is a term generally more familiar to commercial designers, while the POE is more familiar to the residential designer. The concepts covered in this brief discussion are similar for either term.

A POE (or FPE) also provides an additional opportunity to fine-tune a recently completed project. To be more precise, a POE is a comprehensive evaluation and review of a project from the client and interior designer's perspective. By seeking out information on client satisfaction, the designer can often reduce dissatisfaction and stop critical issues from becoming large problems that cannot be easily solved. A postoccupancy evaluation can also assist the designer in streamlining procedures in future projects.

The designer asks questions to try to determine client satisfaction or problem areas with planning and design issues (though not necessarily the aesthetics), furniture and product specification, and other issues that are relevant to the project. However, the kinds of questions that will be important to the evaluation of a residence will be different for those concerning a doctor's suite or restaurant or retail store, for example.

Designers who regularly use POEs develop one or more evaluation forms. These forms are distributed to the employees and management of the commercial space so that the evaluation can be done quickly. The data can be easily tabulated by using a computer-based form. Residential interior designers using POE can create a short questionnaire that can be sent to the client or gone over by the designer with the client.

Of course, there are projects that have not gone very well. Going back to the client to ask about problems is the last thing designers who have had difficulties want to do. Yet it is exactly what they should do in order to return to good relations with the customer and to fix processes and procedures for the future. Interior designers can also prepare internal postproject evaluations that help the designer and firm evaluate processes and procedures from the design firm's point of view.

Postoccupancy and postproject evaluations are additional research tools to assist firms to become better designers and organizations. Becoming better results in better customer service and satisfied clients.

DEVELOPING A RESEARCH PROJECT

Regardless of the reason, the type, or scope of research to be conducted, results improve when the research is done through a systematic process. Careful planning of the research project is critical to gathering the kind of information that will be meaningful, objective, and valid. Just winging it did not get man to the moon or even the design of a hotel or large high-end residence.

This section describes the research process for efforts that go beyond the "standard" research conducted to complete programming and a design project. The steps described apply to many kinds of research you might perform in the design profession regardless of specialty. The steps in the research project process are:

- Define the problem or purpose.
- Plan the research methodology.
- Collect the information or data.
- Analyze the information or data.
- Prepare necessary reports and/or graphics.[8]

Define the Problem

A research project begins with the definition of your *research problem* or needs. Some would say that it begins with a question. Others would say that the research begins with a hypothesis. A *hypothesis* is an assumption based on limited information. Obviously, you need to state what it is you are trying to investigate. Your question may lead you to look for specific information or something more complex. An example of the former is: what were the influences on the development of the Queen Anne style of furniture in America? An example of the latter might be: is there potential to develop evidence-based design research for boutique hotel projects?

Certainly, it is obvious that research activities and methodologies will be different when a student needs to prepare a paper for a class versus what a practitioner might research. It makes sense that the clearer the definition of the research problem, the fewer obstacles will emerge. In some situations, the problem can be clearly defined by trying to project what the end result is to be. Not clearly defining the problem leads to wasted time and misused efforts. An example of an unclear problem statement is the following: "Design an assisted living apartment." It is not very clear or specific because a lot has been left out of the problem. Is this for a couple, an individual, or a prototype for management to be used as a selling tool?

An aid in defining the problem is defining any applicable goals and objectives. You will recall from Chapter 3 that a goal is a broadly stated desired result you wish to achieve. Objectives are more specific and describe what must be done to achieve the goal. "Goals indicate what the client wants to achieve; objectives indicate how to achieve the goals and to what degree."[9] Establishing goals and objectives helps direct any type of research activity, not just for a design project.

Planning the Research

The next step is to plan the methods or systems that will be used to solve the problem. Planning your project helps to keep you focused. You do not start gathering information until you know what kinds of information you will be looking for. Planning is needed to clarify which methods will be used to obtain and subsequently analyze the information.

Research data or information is obtained and considered either primary or secondary data. *Primary data* or a primary data source is considered original. It is primary because it comes from original sources of information, such as a survey provides. Generally, primary data has not been published before. The data obtained by a firm that sends postproject surveys to clients is another example. The information you gather from the client during initial programming is also generally considered primary data.

Information that has already been published or in some way already exists is considered *secondary research data*. Secondary sources are commonly utilized when preparing reports rather than for obtaining new, previously unknown data. When students refer to books to write a paper for a class, they are using secondary data. Another example of secondary data is a review of several issues of the business section of the local paper to look for potential clients. Secondary sources of information might also be included in the development of concept statements.

Secondary source data can also be obtained by manipulating previously collected data. The manager of a design department might research data concerning the productivity of the design staff for the past year by using statistical formulas and historical data on the number of hours worked each week or month by staff members.

Collect the Information or Data—Research Techniques and Methods

The next step is to collect information and/or data. Depending on the research problem, a project might start with the review of existing secondary data. It is almost always helpful to begin with what is already known about a particular problem. It is quite common and even expected for professors, students, and writers, for example, to produce a literature review concerning their specific research problem. A designer often must review building codebooks before beginning design work—an example of data collection as applicable to a design project.

Depending on the research project, collecting the data can be relatively simple and moderately inexpensive or become involved and costly. There are various kinds of research design techniques that can be used to execute the research project (see Table 5.1). Surveys, questionnaires, and observation techniques are discussed in depth, while the other methods are discussed briefly at the end of this section.

The most common research design techniques for the type of research an interior designer might engage are surveys and

TABLE 5.1. The Most Common Types of Research Methodologies

Surveys	Focus groups
Questionnaires	Case studies
Observation	Postoccupancy evaluations
Literature or data reviews	Prototypes
Interviews	Experiments

observation techniques. Let's look at each of these in some detail. **Surveys** are a very common method of obtaining information. They are frequently thought of as *questionnaires* since surveys can be structured using questions. A crucial key to using the survey is careful development of the items or questions that will be included. It is critical that the survey be limited to appropriate and focused items or questions. Surveys can be structured by other means to obtain information without using actual questions. Faulty questions lead to faulty results and information in the final report. Poorly designed questions can also mislead the research into a direction that is not objective.

Surveys require time to develop, the time or cost to distribute to the population—those being surveyed—and the time and cost to analyze the information. Thus, they can be expensive. However, they are also a less expensive way of obtaining information from a large number of respondents versus other research methods.

Surveys are specifically designed to solicit data that might support or refute the problem statement or hypothesis. The survey item beginning on page 106 is a sample instrument. A design firm might use this type of questionnaire to obtain client feedback on past performance or client satisfaction. Large corporations use many types of surveys to determine consumer preferences, marketing effectiveness, and many other topics.

A Sample Survey Instrument Used for an Online or Telephone Survey

Provided by: The American Society of Interior Designers (ASID), Washington, DC.

Sustainable Home Design

We are interested in learning about homeowners' preferences for sustainably designed homes. We would greatly appreciate it if you take a couple of minutes to respond to the questions below. Your answers are anonymous and will be kept strictly confidential.

Question 1

Sustainable home design is design that seeks to conserve energy, reduce waste, and minimize the use of harmful substances and non-renewable resources within the home. Sustainable design is increasingly becoming cost-competitive with standard home designs. If you had a home improvement project planned in the near future, how likely would you be to consider a sustainable design?

☐ Very Likely

☐ Somewhat Likely

☐ Somewhat Not Likely   (please go to Question 4)

☐ Not at All Likely   (please go to Question 4)

☐ Don't Know   (please go to Question 4)

Question 2

If you answered "Very Likely" or "Somewhat Likely" to Question 1, would you consider paying for the services of an interior designer trained in sustainable design in order to have your home meet sustainable design guidelines?

☐ Yes

☐ No   (please go to Question 4)

☐ Don't Know   (please go to Question 4)

Question 3

If you answered "Yes" to Question 3, what percent over the standard pricing would you be willing to pay for these services?

(a) Would you be willing to pay 2 percent over standard pricing?

  ☐ Yes

  ☐ No

  ☐ Don't Know

(b) Would you be willing to pay 5 percent over standard pricing?

  ☐ Yes

  ☐ No

  ☐ Don't Know

(c) Would you be willing to pay 7 percent over standard pricing?

  ☐ Yes

  ☐ No

  ☐ Don't Know

Question 4

Do you believe that a nationally recognized certification stating that your home is designed to these sustainable environmental guidelines would increase the value of your home?

  ☐ Yes

  ☐ No   (please go to end)

  ☐ Don't Know   (please go to end)

Question 5

Would you be willing to pay for a licensed professional to certify that your home was designed to sustainable environmental guidelines?

(a) Would you be willing to pay for such a certification if the fee were approximately $100?

(continued)

☐ Yes

☐ No

☐ Don't Know

(b) Would you be willing to pay for such a certification if the fee were approximately $250?

☐ Yes

☐ No

☐ Don't Know

(c) Would you be willing to pay for such a certification if the fee were approximately $500?

☐ Yes

☐ No

☐ Don't Know

Thank you for completing the survey. Your responses will help us to better meet homeowners' needs in the future.

A survey can be conducted face-to-face in an interview; over the telephone; or mailed. Web-based instruments and email versions of surveys are becoming more prevalent. (Surveymonkey.com has become a popular site to help administer online surveys. Note, however, that the author does not endorse this site. It is mentioned as a resource only.) Electronic surveys require more design time and access to specialized software in order for responses to be easily tallied. You may have already received surveys that were emailed from professional associations and/or vendors.

Participants can be asked to respond in different ways. A common method is to create the survey so that items can be answered by checking off answers, similar to a multiple-choice test. Another is open-ended, allowing the participant to fill in blanks after the item or question. Using face-to-face or telephone interviews permits respondents to expand on answers. A problem with questionnaires that allow for open-ended responses is that they are harder to tabulate.

Observation is another research method. It is considered a type of *empirical research*. You can find many definitions of empirical research, but this one works very well: "empirical is based on, concerned with, or verifiable by observation or experience rather than theory or pure logic."[10]

Empirical research is generally measured research, such as counting the individuals that enter a store. A simple version of the research method of observation occurs when you tour a client's home or office. Observation can help the designer find out many things, such as how the space is used, situational behavior by occupants, and what is in the interior.

It can also be somewhat time consuming and costly, as many variables can be included in the observation besides simple counting. Perhaps the observer also records the gender of the shopper as well as which direction the customer turns when entering. Of course, by using observation, the researcher cannot discover data on such issues as the customer's motivation for coming to the store or opinions about the design or other attributes that will likely be of interest to the client and the designer.

Observational research must be planned like any other research project. You must determine what your research problem involves, get permission from the appropriate authority (in some cases) to conduct the observation, and plan how you are going to record and use the information.

This type of research must be done with the recognition of privacy of those involved or being researched. In a commercial facility, it is not only sensible but good practice to obtain permission of the owner or manager of the facility before beginning any observational research. Security is an issue in many commercial facilities, and it would not be unusual for strangers with clipboards, cameras, and measuring tapes to be confronted by employees.

Observation must be done with some caution. Although we might think that observation is neutral, our powers of observation can be negatively impacted by many factors. Sometimes there is "a tendency to see or hear what we wish to see or hear, selecting and remembering those aspects of an experience that are most consistent with our previous experience and background."[11] Every now and then that information is in conflict with what we already believe or have learned. Perhaps we are distracted with other thoughts. Someone might be talking to us as we are trying to observe and evaluate. Our beliefs and expectations can also impact our observations. These issues need to be controlled when conducting observational research.

Empathic Research

Another type of observational research is empathic research. *Empathy* involves being able to relate to or sympathize with others. In this case, *empathic research* helps businesses find out what customers really want rather than developing products and services that companies choose to offer. It has been receiving attention in the press and in books on consumer behavior and marketing since the late 1990s. Most of the literature discussing emphatic research is focused on product design and product marketing.

Empathic research, being observational, tries to see how buyers actually use products in the buyer's own setting rather than in controlled environments, such as in focus groups. Researchers involved in empathic research believe this type of observation brings truer results. This is because people in a focus group or in a controlled environment will often give the researcher what the researcher wants to know or hear rather than the "truth."

Of course, designers have known for a long time that seeing the client in his or her environment provides better clues to how the client will use the space and what they really want for the interiors. Although a questionnaire can obtain important information for designing a new space, observing the client in his or her current environment adds substance to the questionnaire answers.

By engaging in empathic observational research, a designer might find out indirect positive uses or opinions on a product or service. These are often things about a product or service that the client does not tell to the designer. An example is the increased productivity and pride employees have working in a well-designed and planned environment versus a previously cramped space.

It is important for you to have at least a minimal understanding of the other types of research methodologies. Due to the nature of this text and this chapter, it is not possible to discuss each of these in depth. Following are some brief definitions:

Literature or data review. The researcher investigates published books, articles, and other information to determine what has already been discovered on the topic.

Interview. Part of the survey and questionnaire process previously discussed.

Focus group. A group of individuals are asked about their opinions, feelings, and so on concerning a product, concept, or advertisement, to name the most common.

Case study. An in-depth study of a situation, event, or project in order to determine outcomes, success, or failure.

Postoccupancy evaluation. See the box about "Postoccupancy Evaluations" on pages 99 to 101 for more information.

Prototype. A sample of an item that is under consideration or can serve as a mock-up of an item before full-scale production is started.

Experiment. Controlled test, exploration, or study.

Analyze the Information

Regardless of how the information has been acquired, the data must be analyzed in order for it to be of use to the designer. *Analysis* involves using methods to summarize the data so that it is easier to report and understand by the audience for which it is intended. How the analysis will be done will vary from the method used to gather the information.

Often, the data must be tabulated before it can be analyzed. Obviously, computers are extremely useful in tabulating answers to many questionnaires and surveys. Whenever possible, entering questionnaire answers directly into a computer speeds up tabulation. Manually tabulating results can be done, but it is time consuming and can be expensive.

In analyzing the data, the designer uses his or her experience to look for patterns and details. Assuming you have developed your problem carefully and the method of data gathering was actually designed to gather the information you sought, the analysis is more straightforward. Perhaps a firm wishes to find out if past clients have been satisfied with the design services provided. The obvious pattern to look for is a positive or negative impression of the services.

Some research will also provide statistical information that can be reviewed. Surveys can provide numerous kinds of statistical information. For example, a professional association might want to know how many of its members engage in each design specialty. A survey sent to consumers might try to determine which fee method consumers prefer.

When it becomes apparent that the problem or hypothesis was or was not proven, additional analysis or research might be necessary. Whether or not the hypothesis was verified does not necessarily mean the research was faulty. There may be disappointment in the results, or there may be enlightenment. Which occurs will be a result of the entire research process.

Prepare Reports and/or Graphics

A report of some type, possibly including graphics, such as charts and diagrams, will be necessary to conclude the research project. This can in some respects be considered the synthesis of the information obtained in the research process. In some situations, such as the programming information obtained through one-on-one interviews of the client for a project, a written report might not be prepared.

In many types of research, the more clearly the information is reported, the better it will be utilized. An organized structure is beneficial for any type of report regardless of the audience. Confused structure and language will lead to disappointed readers, whoever they may be. Providing an introduction and explanation of the research method before getting into the results is preferred. If the research is of the type where a literature search was conducted, then it should end with a reference list.

Formal research reporting has a structure that includes an *abstract* and/or introduction that provides a brief overview of the report. A example of an abstract follows. The abstract is followed by research information presented in a format that might need to follow very specific guidelines and concludes with a list of references. For example, a research study submitted to the *Journal of Interior Design* must meet specific guidelines of that journal. You can find these specific guidelines by going to the Interior Design Educators Council web site www.idec.org and tabbing to the Journal.

Example of a Research Abstract Printed in a Journal

Provided by: Caren S. Martin, PhD, FASID, IDEC, University of Minnesota. Published courtesy of the *Journal of Interior Design.*

Rebuttal of the Report by the Institute for Justice Entitled Designing Cartels: How Industry Insiders Cut Out Competition

Abstract

In September 2006, the Institute for Justice published a report entitled Designing Cartels: How Industry Insiders Cut Out Competition (Carpenter). The stated purpose was to examine "titling laws, using the interior design industry as the focus, to stimulate further research in this area and to illustrate what titling laws are and how they function" (p. 1). However, the focus of the report, in concert with the Institute for Justice's lawsuits against existing interior design regulation in New Mexico and Texas, appears to be an attack on the interior design profession.

This paper is a research-supported rebuttal that analyzes Carpenter's findings within two major constructs: 1) interior decoration is not interior design, and 2) the purpose of regulation. The evidence of the Institute for Justice report is examined via principal topics that include the definition of interior design; the relationship of interior design to the health, safety, and welfare of the public; the framework of interior design regulation; the ideology of consumerism; the function of the Better Business Bureau (BBB) as a measurement tool of industry quality; and the idea of "profession" as a construct.

This rebuttal found that Designing Cartels has not succeeded in presenting findings and conclusions that support its intended purpose. It is unfortunate for the public and the interior design profession that this report has been so widespread and used as a way to bolster litigation against the public interest without being examined more closely. Suggestions of the Institute for Justice, if implemented, could compromise the public's health, safety, and welfare.

ASSESSING INFORMATION

Assessing the source of your information is very important regardless of its ultimate use. Naturally, most project information comes from the client and other stakeholders. Other information the designer needs can come from published sources as well as the Internet. Part of the overall responsibility of the critical designer is to assess information and its validity.

The information obtained from the client and other stakeholders is assumed to be reliable. Of course, some stakeholders might have personal reasons for swaying information toward personal agendas. For example, someone who is used to having a private office might try to sway the designer to believe that he or she still requires complete privacy. This could be a problem when management wants to switch private offices to open office systems furniture.

Published sources of information are also considered generally reliable, as most are reviewed by some entity before publication. An example is the codebooks. They are assumed to be reliable as long as the designer is using the right version of the code. An interior designer might need to have more than one version of codebooks on hand, as jurisdictions do not always adopt the newest version.

What information should be trusted when we need to critically think through choices? We start assessing information based on our own experiences. Naturally, parents, teachers, and others we interact with influence us. Books, magazines, and the media also have an influence. It is easy to understand that our own background of learning serves as the strongest source of opinion about the information we continually encounter.

As a critical thinker and as you assess information, it is important to recognize the difference between personal opinion and informed opinion. *Personal opinion* is thoughts and beliefs based on our previous learning and experience. It is based solely on personal judgment. *Informed opinion* is that based on reliable information that generally goes beyond one's own experiences.

Assessing information for research purposes or to help with critical thinking benefit from a process. Regardless of where the information comes from, it is important to evaluate the information to be sure it is appropriate. Of course, the topic of the research or question being investigated has a lot to do with which of these factors might be of greatest importance in your research. The following are key issues to address when assessing information:

- How current is the information?
- Who or what is the source of the information?
- Is it relevant to the issue being investigated?
- Does the information contain bias?

The Internet is a place where anyone can "publish" anything on any topic. A great deal of this information is based on personal opinion and might not be researched by the author. The factors of currency, source, relevance, and bias are especially important to evaluate information obtained from the Internet. A brief discussion concerning assessing information from the Internet concludes the chapter.

Is the Information Current?

Some research projects or questions might be very time sensitive. If you are researching information on how to structure your resume for an immediate job search, you will want very current information to assist you. Should the research be historical in nature, resources that might be some years old would remain relevant. An example of this would be reviewing original archived historical documents. Material on technology, for example, will get "old" very quickly, as technology changes rapidly.

When you are looking at an article, book, magazine, or other print media, the date the information was published is easily determined. The copyright date or date of the issue provides this information.

Statistics and data published in a book or article were likely obtained several months, if not years, before the publication date.

Authors try to keep the information as current as is feasible. If absolutely current information is needed, it can probably be obtained only by primary research activities.

Who or What Is the Source of the Information?

Authors of books and magazine articles are generally reliable sources since the organization that published the material has thoroughly investigated the author. Of course, an author might have a bias related to the topic. That might be difficult for a researcher to discern if the author has not published anything before or is otherwise not known in the subject matter.

Publications themselves will sometimes need to be evaluated relevant to the research question or topic. For example, some news magazines are traditionally conservative (or liberal) in their content, while others are essentially neutral. The focus of the publication thus may indicate a bias or neutrality.

Magazines are slanted toward particular audiences. For example, magazines available only to members of the design industry are called *trade magazines*. Design-focused magazines available to the general public by subscription or on the newsstands are called *consumer* or *shelter magazines*. In the interior design industry, one magazine might appeal to the residential designer and general public, while others are targeted to commercial designers. For example, *Architectural Digest* is a magazine that targets readers who are residential designers as well as the general public. *Healthcare Design* magazine, for example, is available to members of the design/build industry and health care professionals and is not readably available to the general public.

Journal articles, such as those published in the *Journal of Interior Design*, are targeted to educators, design practitioners, and students of interior design. These articles are refereed, which means a group of experts review the proposed materials as part of the consideration process for publication. Although some pieces might be interesting to the general public, they are not intended for the consumer.

Is It Relevant to the Issue Being Investigated?

Another question to ask as you research a source for relevance is whether it addresses the focus of the research. Seems logical, but it is something that can be lost in the search, especially when you are in a hurry. For example, if the issue is what type of wall finishes can be used in a bed-and-breakfast space, the information in the building code may be insufficient since local codes might be more stringent. Both must be reviewed for relevant application.

It can be helpful to consider the level of information that is intended. By that I mean the level of experience, previous knowledge of the subject, and even education. Information that appears basic is generally intended for a novice in the subject. At the other end is a professional or in-depth level of understanding of the information. Someone with little knowledge of how to design a hospital emergency room will have difficulty with a professional level publication on that subject.

When you are researching statistical and precise factual information, check for citations supporting the statistics. Someone who might say, for example, "Thirty percent of all designers charge using an hourly fee," with no citation backing up that information, is most likely providing some sort of personal opinion. Be cautious about using statistics that have no citation. It is also important to check the date of that source. Information that was accurate in 1999 is unlikely to be accurate in subsequent years.

Does the Information Contain Bias?

Generally, someone's personal opinion or a personal (or group) agenda will be biased. If the person providing the information is an "expert" in the subject matter, that personal opinion will likely be acceptable for your research purposes. For example, a designer with significant years' experience in the design of health care facilities writing on health care design is writing from personal and professional experience. However, that person also has likely obtained extensive knowledge about that type of facility design through various kinds of educational exposures.

To see beyond personal opinion, review the information for footnotes, bibliographic citations, or notes concerning sources. You should also look to see if material that is quoted from other sources is actually cited. It is important that direct quotes acknowledge the source of the information. You may wish to return to Chapter 4 and the section on bias for other information on the topic of bias.

You can obtain much assistance on where to look for information and perhaps even its reliability by discussing your research project with a librarian. Reference specialists are among the many people who can help you focus your searches. If you are near a university or college library, it is likely that you will have greater access to higher-quality resource materials. It might be necessary to obtain a "user" or "guest" account at a university library if you are not a student. It is also possible to find information about selecting research sources on the Internet. Enter a university site (.edu) and find the "library" tab. Work your way through the menus to see if you can find information that will help you find resources and even help you to evaluate resources.

ASSESSING INFORMATION FROM THE INTERNET

Caution is suggested when utilizing Internet sources as the major source of information for any research. The same standards should be applied to the information you look for on the Internet as those from traditional sources. You must be sure the information is credible both in content and the source or author. Internet information from sources other than universities and professional organizations is not commonly reviewed or juried before publication on a web site. Remember that anyone is free to have a web page or publish material on any subject on web sites.

Internet information is harder to date accurately. Not all web pages with articles provide a date under the title or otherwise on the page. Some note revision dates so that you can tell if it is up to date or old. A test for the timeliness of Internet information is to check if the internal links on the page still work. If they do not, then it is possible that the information is not current. It should be noted that footnotes, bibliographic citations, or notes concerning sources do not always appear on Internet articles.

Investigating the authorship or source of Internet articles is more difficult. Not all articles contain an author's name as would be found in print media. Here are some clues to help determine authorship: You can research the web site by doing a search on the site or sponsoring organization of the site. Investigate who or what group developed the site and the credentials of the site group and authors. Another clue is whether the web site or author has included a way for you to contact them, even if only by an email. If a name is provided, check for the author's credentials via a short bio or credentials, such as professional association membership. You can also use a search engine to try to find information on the author.

When searching on the Internet, many subject lines that are presented sound right on the topic you are researching due to strategies of online site design. When you see an item that appears valid, read the whole article, as the title might be one to catch attention, but the content does not reflect the title or or is not relevant to your needs. For example, an item that has a title of "Selecting Green Flooring Materials" might be something you need and likely it will contain some information about that topic. It is important to read it critically to be sure it is not more of a sales pitch from a particular vendor than general information on the topic.

Consider the audience of the site when researching on the Internet. Try to determine if the site suits your needs, not general information needs. Legal information on sites for the general public is different than legal information provided on sites from academic law libraries or jurisdictional offices of attorneys general. Complete clarity of the information on what you must do legally in being licensed in your jurisdiction, for example, needs to come from state or provincial government departments, not overview legal sites.

Association web sites have public pages as well as pages for only members. Many vendors have similar distinctions. Some information on a vendor's site can be accessed only by having a special code.

On the Internet, information concerning the web site and author of the articles will help you determine if the information is biased. Some pieces will have links to other sites that might provide an opposing view. Who developed or hosts the site is a clue to potential bias. This will help you see that the author has tried to remain neutral. If advertising is on the page, determine if the advertising might be from a source that could influence and bias the author toward that company's point of view. This advertising could also indicate unofficial sponsorship of the site that might lead you to believe it is biased.

Since it is so easy to go to one of the several search engines to look for information for any research project on the Internet, it is very important that you think critically about the information you find there. Investigate carefully before relying on Internet articles for your research. If you are unsure about the reliability of a source, check with a librarian, professor, or trusted colleague.

CONCLUSION

Research activity is part of the interior designer's everyday tasks. As a critically thinking designer, research must be considered a task that goes beyond the research one does to select products for the project. Research is important to help the designer better understand his or her clients, whether those clients' projects involve a residence or some sort of commercial facility. Research is also important to help the designer be a better designer.

Research methodologies that have begun to impact the work of the designer have been included. Evidence-based design is a methodology that is gaining attention and importance. It will help expand the body of knowledge in design and provide critical improvements in the design of interiors and structures. Empathic research, a form of observational research, has received a lot of additional attention in the press during the late 2000s. This type of research is important to designers to help them make wiser choices in planning structures and interiors.

Yet not all research information is alike. Much is already available in the traditional means of books, journal articles, and magazine articles. Naturally, a great deal of information is provided via the Internet and the millions of postings on web sites. The last section of the chapter discusses some typical ways to assess information to help be sure that what the designer relies on is accurate.

This chapter has provided a brief overview of the research process that takes the designer into research problems beyond the specification of products. These processes are important for all design practitioners, as they provide evidence and/or background information to help the designer make decisions.

FOR DISCUSSION

These discussion items and scenario cases require you to use critical thinking to solve one or more problems. In many of these items and cases, you must take the role of a design practice business owner or a practicing designer. There is no *one* right answer to any of these discussion items or scenarios.

1. A designer prepared the following statement for a research project: "Design three typical apartment schemes for an assisted living facility being built by a developer." This stated problem is not very clear.

   ■ How would you write up a more clearly defined problem statement?

2. What would you want to know from a client in order to begin the design of a living room, a child's bedroom, a small retail store, or a bed-and-breakfast inn? Prepare at least five questions for each of these projects. Why would you ask the questions you have listed?

3. Develop a one-page questionnaire suitable to be used to determine finish preferences of residential clients.

4. Locate a research article from the *Journal of Interior Design*, InformeDesign.org, or another design industry source. Prepare an analysis of the research report, and be prepared to make a presentation on the key points for a class.

5. Review at least two sources for information on evidence-based design other than from this book. Prepare a report on how evidence-based design can be useful to the design profession.

Cases for Discussion

1. A designer's responsibility for an office project involves determining what systems furniture is needed. One way the designer can obtain that information is by observing how employees of a client work. Another is to have the employees complete a questionnaire that helps the designer determine furniture needs. A third is for the client managers to make decisions and pass that information on to the designer.

   Let's assume for the moment that the designer has observed the work, but the client also had the employees complete a questionnaire. The designer prepared schematic plans based on the information from the questionnaire and the observations. The manager's statements contradicted the other information obtained by the designer.

   ■ What does the designer do when the information obtained by the designer does not match that given by the manager?

2. Melody works for a design firm that specializes in hospitality and corporate office facilities. She has specialized in hospitality design for several years and has become very interested in what characteristics of design can result in business excellence for bed-and-breakfast facilities. The firm for which she works

has designed these types of lodging facilities in big cities as well as smaller resort communities. Her firm is also interested in acquiring design contracts for boutique hotels.

Melody has spent time researching information from the design firm's records about the bed-and-breakfast facilities the firm has already designed. She is unsure how to go about developing any additional materials and information that would be applicable to her interest. Her boss is willing to let her do her research, but doesn't know how to encourage this work versus her regular design duties. Melody knows she must both think her way through how to do the research and convince her boss that the time she will spend on this effort will be beneficial to the firm.

- ■ What should Melody propose to her boss as the next steps in this research project?

3. Mary wanted to know how customers were using the spaces in a hotel lobby prior to a remodeling project. She first developed a brief form where someone could check the number and types of users of the spaces in the existing lobby. She stationed an employee in the lobby for a period of time observing the comings and goings of individuals who enter the lobby. This information was important to the design planning decisions that Mary then made to redesign the lobby.

- ■ Develop a simple observational research effort to observe how individuals use a public space.

4. Members of the legislative coalition of a state seeking legal recognition of interior design feel that it would be helpful to have factual information about the support of legislation by designers. They want to develop a research study that would provide valid information that could be used in discussions with the state legislators. After some discussions with a

professor from a local school, they decide to create a questionnaire that will be brief and could easily be incorporated as an
online or direct mail item. They know that the database would
start with members of the state professional associations, but
think it would be useful to have data from designers who are
not affiliated with an association.

■ Develop a questionnaire that could be used to obtain the
kind of information discussed in this case.

■ Determine ways of identifying nonaffiliated interior designers who would also be sent the questionnaire.

NOTES

1. Wayne C. Booth, Gregory G. Colomb, and Joseph M. Williams, *The
   Craft of Research*, 3rd ed. (Chicago: University of Chicago Press,
   2008), 10.
2. David Wang, "Diagramming Design Research," *Journal of Interior
   Design* 33(1): 34.
3. William G. Zikmund, *Business Research Methods* (Fort Worth, TX:
   Dryden Press/Harcourt Brace College, 1994), 7.
4. Ibid.
5. Kirk D. Hamilton and David H. Watkins, *Evidence-Based Design for
   Multiple Building Types* (Hoboken, NJ: John Wiley & Sons, 2009), 9.
6. Ibid., p. 12.
7. Christine M. Piotrowski, *Professional Practice for Interior Designers*,
   4th ed. (Hoboken NJ: John Wiley & Sons, 2008), 716.
8. Adapted from Zikmund, p. 37.
9. Rosemary Kilmer and W. Otie Kilmer, *Designing Interiors* (Fort
   Worth, TX: Harcourt Brace Jovanovich, 1992), 181.
10. *The Oxford American College Dictionary*, (New York: Oxford Univer-
    sity Press, 2002), 443.
11. M. Neil Browne and Stuart M. Keeley, *Asking the Right Questions*,
    9th ed. (Upper Saddle River, NJ: Pearson/Prentice Hall, 2010), 103.

6

Decision Making

Decision making is the end of the problem-solving process. It utilizes reflection, critical thinking, and thought to make a choice. It is rarely done in the context of the singular decision. Even something as simple as deciding to go to the local fast-food restaurant is not done without other decisions. Should I drive or walk? Fries or no fries? Decision making involves making choices. When we choose, we make a decision between two or more possibilities; thus, a *decision* is "a conclusion or resolution reached after consideration; the action or process of deciding something or of resolving a question."[1]

Interior design practice involves numerous decision-making opportunities. These opportunities start with the decision to make an appointment with a client to talk about a potential project. They continue throughout the project. I doubt that any designer has actually counted all the decisions he or she has made during the course of any size of project, but it can be literally thousands.

There are processes and techniques that can be used to help with decision making in the context of the business world. Some personal decision-making tactics are included in this chapter; however, the author leaves that emotionally charged topic to other writers.

MAKING DECISIONS

Many decisions are easy, or at least relatively so. Stopping for a red light is an easy decision. Others are more difficult. Should I take the job with ABC Design firm or with XYZ Interiors? Will the bamboo flooring provide a better sustainable solution, or do I need some other product?

Decisions often involve multiple options. For example, ordering a cup of coffee has become difficult. Do you want a *grande* or *venti*, with milk or fat free, with flavored syrup or an extra shot of espresso? Who would have thought 15 years ago that ordering a cup of coffee would become difficult?

Compounding the problem of making decisions is the vast amount of information that is often researched and considered before a decision can be made. For example, which authority is valid when it comes to building code issues? This is important because the codes for the project location can be different than what is familiar to the designer.

Some people have a hard time making decisions because of the fear of actually making a decision. They may feel that if they make the wrong decision, the consequences will be awkward. This is especially a problem in the workplace where an employee in charge of making a decision may be reluctant or at least overly cautious for fear of being reprimanded or even fired if the result is not satisfactory. Not to decide, however, is a decision.

Then, of course, faulty decisions can have a major impact on the project, the client, and the design firm. A designer may choose to pursue a space plan with certain features. After working on the plan for numerous hours, it might become obvious that those features are not possible. Precious time might have been wasted in pursuit of a solution that in the end did not work. Lawsuits, added financial costs by the firm, bad publicity, and the ruin of a designer's good name can and do happen when bad decisions are made.

Decisions and choices are everyday requirements of the interior designer. Professionals need to know how to evaluate the information that is obtained from various sources to make sure that the decisions they are making are based on sound thinking. Through decision making we learn how to think critically and seek to make our own decisions.

WHAT CONSTITUTES DECISION MAKING?

Interior design is a process involving many steps and applications of information and knowledge involving many decisions. So it would not likely surprise you that decision making is also a process. The process is similar whether one is making a business decision or most any other decision.

Today, you have and will continue to make all sorts of decisions. You could have checked up on people you have an interest in via Twitter; worked on a project; or numerous other activities related to personal concerns, work, or school. You decided to read this book. The fact that you are reading this book constitutes the end of a decision process. Understanding how you got to the "end" is very important. Your decisions can be influenced by past experience with the issue, disagreement with others who are involved, uncertainty, and an authority, such as a boss.

Confidence in decision making comes at least in part from experience. Problem-solving and decision-making situations in interior design are not to be feared but relished, as interior design is full of both of these activities. Becoming more comfortable with the decision-making process will help you make better choices.

Here is a list of the generally accepted steps in the decision-making process, followed by a brief discussion of each step:

- Identify the problem.
- Identify alternative solutions.
- Evaluate the alternatives against some criteria.
- Select the best option by decision or negotiation.
- Implement the best option.
- Evaluate the results of the decision.

Identify the Problem

This step involves clearly recognizing the actual problem. Sometimes more than one issue may be involved, so clarity is beneficial. It is also important at this early stage to try to determine the cause of the problem. Sometimes this is not easy to determine, so talking over the issue not only with the client but with a trusted adviser or colleague can be helpful.

Identify Alternative Solutions

Most problems or situations have more than one solution. In order to make the best decision, it is important to try to identify many options. As was pointed out in Chapter 2, the first solution is rarely the best solution to a design project. That is also the case in the majority of decision-making situations.

Evaluate the Alternatives against Some Criteria

There is always something that impacts the choice—resource availability, quality, and price are only a few criteria. In addition, each possible solution has positive and negative consequences. The criteria used to evaluate the alternative must be something that has importance to the individual or company making the decision, as well as being somehow related to the problem.

Select the Best Option

If careful research is done concerning the alternatives and the evaluation criteria, only one option should rise to the top as the best solution. It will likely be the option that meets the most criteria. In addition, it is likely to be the one that is most realistic, is least costly (if cost is a factor), fits the client's budget, and has the least risk.

Implement the Best Option

This is best begun by considering what the situation will look like when the chosen option is employed. Implementation can be as simple as making a few phone calls. For complex decisions, a full-blown action plan that outlines the needed steps may be required. For a design project, implementation naturally means the development of space plans, furniture layouts, and other required documents.

Evaluate the Results of the Decision

Simple decisions don't often involve "postdecision evaluation"—though sometimes that might not be a bad idea. It was easy to decide to have dessert, but the "postdecision" evaluation might be the realization that the extra calories are a problem. Complex decisions should be evaluated and even monitored. It is an excellent and proper way to determine if the decision brought the desired results. Depending on the type of decision that was made, it also can be very useful to evaluate the decision so that a similar situation in the future can be resolved with a much quicker decision process. Of course, verifying that the problem was actually solved by the decision is part of the evaluation portion of the process.

Obviously, not all decisions we make are undertaken consciously utilizing the described detailed process. Many of our decisions are intuitive, based on experiences related to the issue at hand. Hopefully, your more important decisions are not based solely on intuition. Experience does play a major part in decision making. The more you know about the problem or opportunity at hand, the better your decision will be. It is easy to understand that an interior designer experienced in the design of retail stores will make better decisions on how to plan a project for a boutique store than someone with limited retail design experience.

DECISION-MAKING STRATEGIES

It is rare that we make decisions in a vacuum. In all likelihood, something has provided lessons that help each of us with decision making. Those lessons come primarily from the experience of making decisions, whatever the context. We might also learn decision making by watching and learning from others: parents, teachers, work colleagues, and friends have a strong influence in teaching us how to make decisions.

Intuition is another way to consider experience-based decision making. Intuitive thought is fast, easy, and from the "gut." Unfortunately, intuition is often unreliable and incorrect when decisions are made based on little experience or evidence. We do not learn interior design by intuition. We also do not or should not make decisions concerning interiors projects or other critical problems and situations based on intuition.

There are several specific strategies to help make decisions in business situations. Many decisions are made by trial and error.

Strategies that are more complex but provide effective results for complex problems are what-if analysis and cost-benefit analysis. When a critical decision must be made, one of these strategies might be helpful.

Trial and Error

Many decisions are frankly made on the basis of trial and error. According to the dictionary, *trial and error* is "a finding out of the best way to reach a desired result or a correct solution by trying out one or more ways or means and by noting and eliminating errors or causes of failure."[2] It certainly can work. But for the most part, trial-and-error decision making takes longer than any other process.

Space-planning solutions do result from what might be defined as trial and error. Using the information obtained through programming, designers begin "trying" to find a feasible floor plan. When it doesn't seem right, the designer tries modifications to parts of the plan until a workable solution is found. It is effective only when reasonable programming information has been gathered and analyzed to help direct the designer to a feasible solution.

Applying trial-and-error decision making to business decisions can be costly. For example, a design firm owner forgoes marketing planning and simply tries to obtain new clients by paying for advertising in a newspaper. She tries an ad, expecting quick results, but nothing happens. So she tries an advertisement in a magazine. Still nothing happens. She hears from a colleague that a direct mail effort can get new business. Without researching how that works, she develops a mailing and distribution of brochures. Once again, the result is less than expected. Trial and error didn't work because no research and planning went into the whole marketing effort.

Trial-and-error decision making is not the best way to find the solution to many problems the designer will encounter in critical thinking and problem solving. One of the following techniques can be more effective in many situations.

What-If Analysis

"What if we use a fixed fee for this project rather than an hourly fee?" said Sam, the manager of a small design firm, to one of his project managers. "What if we refocus our firm to work in the niche of small hospitality projects?" considers another design manager. Challenging a decision by altering one of the component parts of that decision can bring out some interesting results. Most frequently, that component is a numerical value, such as mentioned in the opening comment, though it can be used for any type of situational analysis, such as in the latter example. This decision-making strategy is referred to as *what-if analysis.*

Specifically, what-if analysis is a decision-making technique that asks questions of a situation. The questions seek to find alternatives that are better than the original condition. This type of analysis has less risk than forging ahead with a decision that has not been thought out. By raising appropriate questions, it forces the designer to think through the situation or problem.

This type of analysis is also sometimes referred to as sensitivity analysis, or *situational brainstorming*. It is a very useful way to think through problems or hypothetical situations. For example, "What if the state government requires designers to charge sales tax on design services?" Another example could be "What if we spend 50 percent of our expected profits on marketing this coming year?" As you can see, many kinds of scenarios, data, or information can be questioned using what-if analysis. The sample What-If Analysis illustration on page 137 shows what might happen by manipulating one or more data points. This illustration gives you an idea of what a what-if analysis report would look like.

When used with a scenario or situation, the brainstorming is best when it is "no holds barred," meaning all reasonable ideas and information should be brought forward but remain focused on the primary premise. Questions need to be answered as they are raised before a decision point is reached. The goal, of course, is to find a positive solution to the premise before actually implementing something without research or thought.

Sample What-If Analysis

What if we are able to increase revenues by 5, 10, or 20 percent?

Last year's gross revenue	$502,500
Increase by 5%	$527,625
Increase by 10%	$552,750
Increase by 20%	$603,000

What if we lose revenues at the levels of 10, 15, and 20 percent?

Decrease by 10%	$452,250
Decrease by 15%	$427,125
Decrease by 20%	$402,000

Sample questions that will impact the what-if analysis:

What must the company do to increase revenues by 5, 10, or 20 percent?

What must the company do to prevent decreases in revenue by 10, 15, or 20 percent?

What if our operating expenses increase at half the rate of the revenue increase? Assume our overhead expenses last year were $375,000.

What would the results be if you changed all the above by 3 percent at each level?

How would that impact operating expenses?

What-if analysis involving numeric information was popularized by the makers of data analysis and spreadsheet software. By changing individual components of numeric data, one can formulate potential results without incurring costs other than the time it takes to run the analysis. A best-option decision can then be made.

Cost-Benefit Analysis

A decision-making strategy that is useful for decisions involving financial data is *cost-benefit analysis*. According to the *Encyclopedia of Business Ethics and Society*, "Cost-benefit analysis (CBA) is a rational choice framework for identifying the best or most profitable option a decision maker can undertake."[3] In a sense, this is similar to the technique of listing pros and cons of many kinds of decisions; however, in this case, you include the costs factors of options. Cost-benefit analysis is not limited to financial data analysis, although it is the typical use.

A manager gathers information on the costs of a projected problem and attempts to define the benefits that might exist. Ideally, the value of the benefits is determined in quantifiable terms. In this sense, benefits are any positive factors that might result. In many situations, the costs are one-time costs related to the problem. The benefits are generally more long-term financially. In addition, when a purchase or hiring decision is the kind of problem being considered, the time factor has to be included in the data. This is considered a payback time factor, also known as the break-even point.

For discussion, let's look at this example. Perhaps the workload of the design group has increased so significantly that the owner is considering hiring a new staff member. The sample Cost-Benefit Analysis illustration on page 140 shows approximate costs and financial benefits of hiring a new staff member. This illustration gives you an idea of what a cost-benefit analysis report would look like. The manager should gather cost information to include these types of items:

POTENTIAL COSTS (OR PROBLEMS)
- Possible salary costs per month of the new employee
- Possible employee benefit costs per month
- Costs of potential new furniture items or space for the employee
- Training time cost of the owner or other employee
- Time lost by owner in the hiring process

BENEFITS OF HIRING A NEW EMPLOYEE
- Less stress on existing employees to get work accomplished
- Capability to take on more clients and projects
- Potential ability to work on a new specialty familiar to a new employee
- New employee may bring his or her past clients to the firm
- New employee's reputation may add to firm reputation

Large design firms use cost-benefit analysis more frequently than smaller interior design firms to look at the financial costs and benefits of construction techniques and products. The interior design firm can find benefit using this method when considering purchasing equipment for the office or hiring staff and for other business decisions. It can be useful for firms designing and specifying projects where the costs of different but similar products are being considered. One example is the evaluation of the cost and benefit of purchasing products up front or waiting to purchase some goods at a later time. The costs and benefits will be fairly easy to determine when the prices of the goods at a future time can be forecasted.

Sample Cost-Benefit Analysis

Potential Costs of Hiring a New Employee

Salary cost of new employee	$ 45,000
Employee benefits costs	$13,500
New furniture	$4,000
Nonbillable training time	$5,000
Nonbillable time for boss for hiring process	$3,600
Total anticipated costs	$71,100

Potential Benefits of Hiring New Employee

Potential revenue from new clients	estimate	$ 51,000
Reduced overtime for existing staff	estimate	$5,000
Improved billable time for owner	estimate	$10,000
Improved accuracy of work	estimate	$10,000
Total estimated dollar benefits		$76,000
Estimated possible revenue benefit		$4,900

Please note that the numerical items in this example do not take into consideration the full value and impact of operating and overhead expenses.

WHY WE MAKE WRONG DECISIONS

Too often, decisions are made by clients, a design business, or designers without careful consideration and useful research. Wrong decisions can be costly. Not all decisions are good or, shall we say, result in positive outcomes. Making decisions is difficult for many people, sometimes with consequences that are not very welcome.

Let's look at a somewhat simple non-design example. It does not make good sense to buy a television today on the spur of the moment without research. There are so many features involved besides size. Brands have different reputations for reliability. Then there are technical factors to consider: should it be an LCD, LED, or 3D, and how many inputs may be needed are only a few characteristics of this seemingly simple product decision. Wrong decisions can be expensive when the chosen television does not provide what you wanted.

Now let's look at a design project example. Clients like to get involved in decisions for small medical suites even when they have no design training. Many times, they select upholstery fabric that they have seen in a residential setting and insist that the interior designer use this residential fabric on seating for the waiting room and exam room chairs. If the designer is not highly experienced in commercial design, he may be quite willing to agree that the fabric is appropriate and specify it for the office chairs. Unfortunately, a residential-grade upholstery fabric will not hold up to the wear-and-tear of an office environment. In addition, depending on the code requirements for the office suite space, the residential upholstery may not meet the fire code requirements.

Wrong decisions are generally easy to avoid when enough information is sought beforehand. Finding quality information starts with understanding the problem inherent in the decision. Rushes to decisions and deciding by the "seat of your pants" are not good practice. It is unlikely that you would decide which school to go to for your interior design training without some research. That same caution should be applied to the decisions you make for clients and other business and personal decisions.

An important point to make is that many decisions are made based on emotions. Many situations are or can be emotionally charged. Who to vote for to be governor of your state or determining to continue working with a client you do not particularly like are examples. Then again, the emotional decision may be one made when the "decider" is not having a great day or is upset. Many look back on what turns out to be a bad decision and realize that the decision was made when the person was in a bad mood or simply made a hasty decision in order to just get it over with.

It is important to take the necessary time and include clarity of purpose when making decisions. A good decision can have lifelong positive consequences—and a bad one can have lifelong negative consequences. The following list provides several reasons why we make wrong decisions. Keep these in mind before you make a wrong decision.

- We don't take the time to ask the right questions.
- We worry about being second-guessed.
- Personal or business distractions.
- Investigation lacks due diligence and adequate depth.
- Our ego tells us we already know the answer.
- We don't want to admit we don't know.
- Minimal skill level of decision making.
- Avoidance and procrastination.
- Passion for the first answer or "great idea" fogs the ability to see potential problems.

Striving to make the right decision is how we all want to be known. No one wants to be known for repeatedly making bad decisions. We always hope, at least, to make the correct decision that leads to positive outcomes. Entry-level designers will learn quickly that bad decisions have a price. Thus, learning decision-making skills is one more task that must be added to the briefcase of skills and knowledge for the designer. It should not take a failing grade or job loss to determine that good decision making is essential.

CONCLUSION

Whether the decision facing you involves the work you are doing with clients, assignments in class, duties required by the boss, or personal choices of any kind, you want to make the "right" decision. Thinking critically is part and parcel of decision making. Without good decision-making skills and thinking critically, many decisions are likely to turn out to be wrong decisions, or certainly cause some sort of negative result.

Coming to a decision is also the end of the problem-solving process. Everything you do to prepare yourself to make a decision hopefully leads you to a positive conclusion. Most of the time that will be true. But reality says that sometimes you will still be wrong. That's OK as long as you also learn something from that wrong decision.

Better problem solving and decision making is accomplished using the types of techniques discussed in this chapter. Taking the time to research the problem and obtain as much information as possible—or at least as practicable—results in better decisions. Remember that learning to think critically and making good decisions happens gradually.

FOR DISCUSSION

These discussion items and scenario cases require you to use critical thinking to solve one or more problems. In many of these items and cases, you must take the role of a design practice business owner or a practicing designer. There is no *one* right answer to any of these discussion items or scenarios.

1. The staff of XYZ design firm includes four experienced designers, one design assistant, an office manager, and the owner. As needed, an extra person who is proficient in computer

assisted design (CAD) is used on a contract basis. In the past four months, there has been a slowdown in the number of new clients and new projects. One of the senior designers has been working only part time due to an ill relative whom she must help care for. Although everyone in the office seems busy, revenues have been going down, and now there is a cash flow problem to pay the rent and other operating expenses.

- Describe the problems that appear to exist in this firm.

- Describe at least three alternatives that would solve this situation.

- Select and defend an option that would improve the situation without losing any employees.

2. If the client is unyielding in his insistence on using design concepts that the designer believes to be poor design, how far should the designer go to try to convince the client of his "wrong" opinion?

3. Your client has been wavering concerning the fabric sample you recommended for the dining room chairs for a midpriced Italian restaurant. When you met with him today, he showed you a patterned fabric that he said his wife found in a local furniture store. It is closer to the color concept that he had described to you at the beginning of the project, and he says it is five dollars a yard cheaper than the one you are suggesting. You can tell that the fabric will not hold up for the dining room chairs based on what he told you during the programming interview.

- How would you approach solving this conflict?

4. Using the scenario style of what-if analysis, (a) develop a scenario to help a design firm market to small retail store owners; (b) determine ways to improve the design of independently owned hotels in resort communities in a particular state (of your choosing). Be sure you provide reasons for your choices.

5. What is the difference between trial-and-error decision making and what-if analysis?

6. A client has asked you to provide a proposal to design a retail store that sells women's clothing. You are very interested in getting this project because the client has mentioned that she plans to open five more stores in the coming 18 months. She also mentioned she was very dissatisfied with the designer who did the store in a neighboring community 20 miles away that opened six months ago.

   The store she wants you to design is located across town in an upscale area. The project would involve the design of the interior shell—partitions as needed, all surfaces, the design of display cases and cabinets, color selections, and lighting design. The target date for move-in and opening is October 1, nine months from the date you met with the owner.

   An issue for you is that you would need to hire a lighting consultant, since your experience with retail lighting has never included lighting design to the extent you believe it will be needed.

   - Prepare a list of the questions the client needs to answer in order to provide a proposal.

   - Prepare a list of questions you must answer in order to determine if you should take this project.

7. Be prepared to share what could be thought of as a bad decision that you made. Explain the situation and the decision. Then describe the results of that bad decision. What did you learn from the experience? If faced with a similar situation again, what would you do differently? How can you use this experience to help you make better decisions in the future?

   Also be prepared to discuss a good decision in the same way.

Cases for Discussion

1. Timothy received a phone call from the project manager at the ABC office complex. The manager was quite irate over the progress of the installation of the furniture for a project Timothy had designed. It is safe to say that the manager read Timothy the "riot act" on how disruptive the installation has been on the manager's staff. Employees had packed up their files and other materials as requested and approved for the install. It was to take only two workdays plus one weekend day. The install is now in its fifth day, with more than half of the employees in the project area unable to work—or even find their boxes of materials. The design firm owner has put Timothy in charge of working with the client in order to satisfy the client.

   ▪ What situations or issues could be involved in causing the delays in installation?

   ▪ What can be done to resolve the situation with ABC?

   ▪ Discuss the positives and negatives of each option offered above.

2. Janice is a designer for a firm that specializes in corporate and professional offices. She has worked at the firm for four years. Her boss, Steve, was designing a doctor's medical suite. Janice has not been involved in this project previously. On Tuesday, Steve told her that she was accompanying him to the client meeting with the doctor. "I need you to take over the project, as I am going to be working on a new project out of town." He quickly explained where he was with the project. Later that day, she went with him on the appointment.

   Upon arrival at the doctor's house, Steve simply introduced Janice as another designer in the firm. Steve proceeded to go through the plan with the doctor and his wife. Some minor changes were noted, but the doctor was pleased with the over-all space plan and furniture plan. He was also satisfied with the specifications explained by Steve. No samples were shown, though color ideas were discussed.

The client seemed quite happy with the progress of the project. Just before leaving, Steve said, "Doctor Jones, Janice is going to be taking over this project. I am going to be out of town on another project for the next two months. She is very ex-perienced, and I'm sure she will work very well with you to complete the office. If needed, she can contact me by email."

Dr. Jones and his wife looked a bit stunned with this news, and the doctor said, "Well, I'm surprised about this. You're sure you can't complete the work?"

"Janice will need to complete the project. As I said, I'll be gone. In fact, I'm leaving Thursday of this week. I'll actually be out of the country for the two months," said Steve. He then hurriedly made excuses to leave for another appointment.

The next day the doctor called Steve to cancel the contract. He also said, "I hired you to do this project, not some assistant. Your name is on the contract, and I think you have breached our agreement. I am going to call my attorney."

■ You are Steve. What would you do?

■ What would you do if you were Steve's boss?

3. There were three emails on Marc's computer that were par-ticularly challenging. Two were from clients who stated that they had seen Marc's web site and were interested in talking to him. The third was from a client who was recommended to Marc by a former client. All three mentioned that they were looking for a designer to work with them on their planned sec-ond homes in different locations in Marc's area. They also all indicated that they lived out of town and would be in the area

for only a few days. Marc, however, was planning a trip out of town himself the week the clients would be in the city. It was a combined vacation and business trip that he could not cancel.

None of the potential clients left a phone number to reach them. The only way to contact the potential clients was through the Internet. He really wanted to at least meet with all three, as he never liked to turn down any opportunity to meet with a potential client. Not wanting to put off any of these potential clients, Marc was trying to decide what to do.

■ How would you handle this decision if you were Marc?

4. Alice worked in residential interior design for eight years. Part of that time she worked at a furniture store and spent three years at a small design studio. At the studio, she began specializing in kitchen designs. Alice is now considering going out on her own and totally focusing on kitchen and bath design. Alice wants to have her business in a small commercial office space located near several cabinet shops and a major appliance showroom.

■ Develop a list of issues she must investigate before she makes the decision to actually open her own office or remain where she is.

NOTES

1. *The Oxford American College Dictionary* (New York: Oxford University Press, 2002), 355.
2. Philip Babcock Gove, ed., *Webster's Third New International Dictionary* (Springfield, MA: Merriam-Webster, 1993), 2439.
3. Robert W. Kolb, ed., *Encyclopedia of Business Ethics and Society*, Vol. 1 (Thousand Oaks, CA: Sage, 2008), 522.

7

Ethical Decision Making

News reports have repeatedly publicized examples of dubious ethical behavior. The Enron Corporation scandal in 2001 led to that corporation's bankruptcy and left thousands without jobs and corporate officers in jail. More recently, the banking industry seemed to use questionable tactics to allow the home mortgage industry to implode with bad loans. This particular ethical scandal had a devastating effect on the design-build industry and interior design profession.

Temptations exist for designers as well. Sometimes, for some reason, an individual or company may decide to turn their head from ethical behavior and decision making. It might be a designer ignoring certain building code requirements in hopes that a code official does not notice. The temptation could be a "special incentive" to specify a particular product. Or a student might steal a design idea from a colleague. Regardless of your position in the design-build industry, clients expect you to behave in an ethical and responsible manner.

But how is ethics defined? According to Miller and Jentz, *ethics* in a business context is "a consensus of what constitutes right or wrong behavior in the world of business and the application of moral principles to situations that arise in a business setting."[1] *Ethical behavior* and ethical standards define "right from wrong" behavior for a profession or group. It is important to point out that part of the standard criteria to define a profession is a requirement for a code of ethics that can be enforced on members.[2]

The interior design profession and the design-build industry are sometimes thought of as very small compared to many other industries. But it is large enough that if someone makes a decision that has serious consequences, the word gets around. Ethical behavior and ethical decision making creates strength and validation for all who are part of the profession. And, by the way, it is also just plain good business practice.

THE IMPORTANCE OF ETHICAL DECISION MAKING

Chapter 6 extensively discussed decision making and the decision-making process. You might ask how ethical decision making is any different from what was discussed in that chapter. This comment might help you with that problem:

> Ethical decision making is a cognitive process that considers various ethical principles, rules, and virtues or the maintenance of relationships to guide or judge individual or group decisions or intended actions. It helps one determine the right course of action or the right thing to do and also enables one to analyze whether another's decisions or actions are right or good. It seeks to

answer questions about how one is supposed to
act or live.[3]

As the general public becomes aware of businesses and individuals behaving in dubious ways, they become less trusting of design professionals as well. Although lapses of ethical behavior, unfortunately, exist in interior design, they are infrequently publicized. Professional associations will report serious breaches of ethics to the association membership via association web sites and newsletters. But it is unlikely that an unethical designer's name will appear on CNN. Many clients think all service providers and sellers are only out for themselves. Is it any wonder that the public is even more wary of service providers who do not meet their obligations?

Designers who are members of the American Society of Interior Designers (ASID), International Interior Design Association (IIDA), or any of the other professional associations are required to abide by a code of ethics. Even those designers who are not in professional associations are likely to be required to meet ethical standards, since jurisdictions that have some sort of design legislation generally require adherence to a code of ethics. Large design firms and designers working for corporations as employees are also required to abide by a code of conduct or ethics. Yet it should be understood that clients expect ethical behavior from all individuals involved in our industry, not just those in an association or working in a regulated jurisdiction.

Borrowing from the *codes of ethics* for ASID and IIDA, association codes set down standards of behavior related to clients, others in the profession, laws of the jurisdiction, and the general public. In addition, ethics also involves an individual's moral compass. Regardless of codified standards, everyone and every company in our industry should embrace ethical decision making and behavior.

Our electronic world creates the opportunity for good and bad deeds to be known around the world. News travels quickly via the Internet, text messaging, and even the traditional medias. Always keep in mind that a satisfied client might tell a few people about her positive experience with a designer while an unsatisfied client tells everyone! Be sure that the decisions you make and the way you conduct yourself in your professional life will not be something that makes the 6 o'clock news or even someone's Twitter page.

You can obtain the code of ethics of ASID and/or IIDA by going to their web sites: www.asid.org and www.iida.org. It is necessary to check with your registrar of contractors or other regulatory body for the code of ethics that will apply in regulated jurisdictions.

An Outline for Ethical Decision Making

Sources: Adapted from Deborah H. Long, *Ethics and the Design Professions* (Washington, DC: National Council for Interior Design Qualification, 2000), 48; and Luis R. Gomez-Mejia, David B. Balkin, and Robert L. Cardy, *Management,* 2nd ed. (New York: McGraw-Hill, 2005), 113.

- What is the ethical problem?
- Who is affected by the decision?
- What are the facts related to the problem?
- Who has the most to gain by the decision?
- Are there legal issues that might impact this decision?
- What are the consequences of making the decision?
- Is there someone you can talk to who can help with the decision?
- Accept responsibility for the decision.

BUSINESS VERSUS ETHICAL CONFLICTS

There can be numerous reasons why someone behaves in an un-ethical manner. Conflicts between business goals and ethical de-cision making are our focus here. For example, when a designer is having difficulties, he or she may be challenged to remain solidly within the bounds of ethical and legal grounds. Even in good economic times, some individuals are challenged as greed and self-interest take over. Let's briefly look at some examples of these conflicts.

Brown and Sukys comment on key reasons that people some-times behave unethically. First, they might do so because they figure they can get away with it. It might even be a "well, ev-erybody does it, so why shouldn't I" attitude. A second reason is that they place their own self-interest ahead of ethical decision making. Third, they have developed a careless attitude.[4]

In the first situation, a designer has to be careful about thinking, "If everyone else does it, what harm is there if I do, too?" Do you always come to a complete stop at a stop sign or before making a right turn on red? Many people don't because they figure they can get away with it. Perhaps a designer has frequently charged clients for a few extra yards of fabric to be sure there is enough to do the job. Everybody does that. Harmless enough if that extra fabric is given to the client, but unethical if the designer keeps it and uses it for his own purposes.

In a case of ethics versus self-interest, maybe the designer blames someone else that work promised by the designer is not done in time or within budget. She does this because she is embarrassed that she did not meet the agreed deadline and budget. Here is another example: Perhaps a student includes design work in her portfolio reworked by another individual. Upon interviewing, the student portrays the work as her own, knowing full well that her skills do not match those shown in the portfolio.

Issues of *self-interest* take many forms. Here's another example: A client brings Jane boards and plans obviously prepared by a designer from another firm. Jane decides to quote prices for the goods shown without checking with the other designer to see if the client has canceled the agreement with the first designer. Jane is operating in a manner of self-interest rather than ethics.

Careless attitudes can easily result in ethical lapses, for example, a designer who does not keep good time records, even though billing by the hour might falsify his time. That kind of behavior can lead to overbilling. He might think, "How is the client going to know I worked only six hours on the drawings rather than the eight I billed him for?" Some designers say that it is not always easy to keep accurate time records when someone is busy with five or six or more projects at once. "Did I go to the carpet vendor for Mr. Jones's office or Ms. Smith's summer home?" a designer might ask himself. However, the client who is billed by the hour expects accurate time billings. There is no excuse for poor time record keeping. Good time record keeping is an easy habit to achieve, especially with all the electronic means of recording time.

Unethical behavior also happens because of greed. It is common for vendors to give designers a *referral fee*—sometimes called a commission—when the designer purchases or specifies goods from the vendor. That fee is often paid to the designer even if the client buys the goods directly from the vendor rather than through the designer. Designers defend these referral fees as a source of revenue. Association codes of ethics require that these extra fees be disclosed to the client.

But what happens if the designer demands such a fee from a vendor who may be desperate to make a sale? Perhaps the design firm simply works out a special deal with a vendor so that this firm gets a bigger discount for a large order. Is this unethical greed or good business?

It is not altogether uncommon that ethical practice and decision making bump up against legal issues. Yet let's be clear about this: ethics and the law are not the same thing. There are numerous situations where behavior that is considered unethical is not considered illegal. Conversely, there are numerous legal requirements that are not necessarily considered ethics issues. It is critical for designers to be familiar with the laws regarding business practice in his or her jurisdiction, since some of these issues will also raise ethics concerns.

An important example concerning this problem pertains to some states' requiring designers who sell architectural finishes and other architectural products to have a contractor's license. Designers who choose not to obtain the license—whether by ignorance of the law or ethical deficiency—and continue to directly bill clients for goods covered by the law are behaving in conflict with ethics and the law. Certainly, revenue is produced by these sales—a business goal—while neglecting to obtain the proper license is unethical and illegal. Bad decisions can easily come back to haunt the designer who might not only be charged with an ethics violation, but could be in trouble legally.

Of course, most practitioners are not unethical. Interior design is a deeply personal profession where clients—regardless of the type of space—must trust designers to be professional businesspeople and expect them to make ethical decisions in the interest of the client. They also must trust the designer, since the designer—often a stranger to the client—will learn confidential information about the client. Designers need this trust to do their jobs effectively. Behavior that is unscrupulous to one or more clients will likely lead them to tell many people when a designer behaves badly. Additional information about the issue of privacy is located on pages 156 to 157.

Most people are not dishonest in their business dealings. Sometimes a wrong decision is made under stress or anxiety that might not even be related to the situation at hand. When ethics and ethical decision making conflict with business goals, the designer should always be sure he or she is continuing on an ethical track. It is in the best interests of all practitioners, students, and those engaged in the interior design industry to work in an ethical manner. Those who do not do harm to us all.

Privacy

In today's world, where it seems that everyone knows everything about everyone else—or can easily find out—privacy is a critical issue. Privacy issues arise concerning a client, a firm, and the individual designer's right to privacy.

Clients provide a substantial amount of confidential and personal information to an interior designer in order for that project to be completed. Private family information is learned when programming questioning is conducted for a residence. Business operations information that a competitor might want to know is frequently shared with the interior designer for many kinds of commercial interiors projects. Some commercial clients may even require that the interior designer sign a *confidentiality agreement*—a legally enforceable agreement not to reveal information—before the project begins.

When research is conducted via surveys, questionnaires, or other means, the respondents expect privacy. They expect that the information provided will be held in confidence or at least not revealed except as needed by the project requirements.

The interior designer also owes a duty to keep confidential information about his or her employer. This can include the names of the clients and projects in process, financial information, methods and manners of pricing services or products sold to clients, and other information private to the company.

Designers must be careful about photographing projects and then using the photos for advertising purposes. For most non-publishing situations, a simple clause in the design contract informing the client that the designer might take photographs during and after the project is sufficient. However, if the designer chooses to include photos for marketing purposes, such as articles in magazines or brochures, the designer should obtain a separate signed release from the client.

In addition, there are federal laws related to privacy of individuals. It is thus important to keep the information you obtain about clients protected from theft, distribution, or even casual conversation.

CLIENT EXPECTATIONS

Clients hire interior designers because we have the expertise they do not possess, although this is but one reason. They go to designers to receive help with whatever the type of interior and expect that they will be treated fairly regardless of affiliation or regulation. Clients do not necessarily approach and work with one interior designer over another because one must abide by a code of ethics while the other does not. Many clients do not even know the difference between an affiliated or regulated designer versus one who is not. They hire designers because they need our help and expect honesty and care in that relationship.

Clients hire a designer to create the interiors that will satisfy the client's needs and wants. It is unfortunate that, too often, designers specify products based on the designer's need to control the project rather than satisfying the client's needs. It is, after all, their home, their business. Is this unethical? Perhaps. Failing to listen to the client, failing to design based on his or her wishes, and exceeding the budget are all ways that the designer falls short in his obligations to the client.

Designers are expected to act in the best interests of the client. Moral right or wrong behavior must be within basic practice in the industry. This is not a choice or a concept of needing to behave ethically only if mandated; it is an imperative required of everyone involved in this industry. When designers do not act in the best interests of the client, everyone in the industry is hurt. Have you had the experience of working with a client who questions your every move and idea and generally gives you the feeling that they think you are trying to cheat them? Perhaps it was because they had previously worked with a designer who behaved in a questionable manner toward them.

Clients initiate most ethics violation complaints. They see it as a way to redress their complaints when a designer does not try to solve the dispute between the parties. Ethics violations are also brought to an association's attention by designers. A description of the process for filing an ethics complaint and any subsequent procedures is available on the web sites of associations.

CONCLUSION

Fortunately, most ethical decisions and dilemmas in interior design practice do not involve life-or-death consequences. They can and do involve situations in which the designer's reputation can be harmed, a financial consequence can be involved, or certainly embarrassment can occur. Each designer must be able to come to his or her own conclusions concerning his or her ethical decision making. And that requires designers to be prepared to explain their reasons for their decisions and accept responsibility for them.

As an interior designer, you will have both personal and professional values that will impact your decision making. Your personal beliefs about truth, honesty, fair-mindedness, and similar concepts might come up against the stresses of the job. Sometimes the stress to obtain projects, and design and specify in the interests of the client versus self-interests, pushes individuals to make decisions that are less than ethical.

Some might argue that ethical decisions can best be made when the decision produces the least harm and the most good and is also fair to all parties involved. If you design in the best interests of your client, you are doing the most good and the least harm not only to your client, but also yourself and the company you work for.

There are many old sayings about ethical behavior. One goes like this: never do anything that you wouldn't want to show up in your local newspaper. In today's electronic world, it might also be wise to remember not to do anything that you wouldn't want to see reported on an Internet site.

FOR DISCUSSION

These scenario cases require you to use critical thinking to solve one or more problems. In many of these items and cases, you must take the role of a design practice business owner or a practicing designer. There is no *one* right answer to any of the scenarios. It would be helpful to obtain a copy of the code of ethics from either ASID or IIDA by going to their web site for these discussion cases.

1. After working for a busy design firm, Clara decided it was time to open her own office. She spent considerable time debating the ramifications of going out on her own versus staying with her current employer. Yet Clara was becoming dissatisfied with the financial arrangement and annoyed by the fact that the owner maintained a level of design control over projects.

   One client had returned to Clara to have her design a boutique bed-and-breakfast in another city. However, when the owner heard about the project, he took it over, relegating Clara to a supporting role. When this happened, Clara told the client that she wanted to start her own firm, and subsequently the client canceled the project with Clara's boss so that he could work with Clara when she started her own firm. Clara promptly left the firm, even with three other projects in the works.

   ■ Be prepared to discuss whether Clara or the boss behaved in a manner contrary to professional ethics.

2. Albert was hired to design a home office for a client, using the garage as the office space. Albert's office was located in a

city 50 miles from the client's home. The project was located in a community known for strict adherence to codes, and the house was in a gated community with a strict homeowners' association. The project involved adding mechanical systems to the space, not simply painting and adding furniture. There were problems with the contractor hired by Albert to do the mechanical work as well as the drywall and painting. The electrician who was to do the installation of the lighting kept giving excuses for the due date of the fixtures. In addition, Albert invoiced the client for work that was not complete and demanded payment. Due to these major issues—and others—the client has threatened to file an ethics complaint against Albert for his mishandling of the project.

- Be prepared to discuss the problems that exist in this situation and provide a method of resolving the problems.

3. Whenever David felt he had some free time at work, he would jump on Facebook or a blog group he belonged to that focused on a nonwork-related hobby he had. Talking to a colleague at a different firm who also got on Facebook at work, David figured he spent about an hour a day in this way. His friend said he probably spent even more time per day on Facebook since they were slow at his company. Because David had to account for all his time at work, he put the time he spent on Facebook down as "house time," which was nonbillable time.

- Discuss the ethical implications of David's behavior.

4. Is it ethical to require the client to pay additional fees for design work that is yet to be done and refusing to do those services until the extra fees are paid?

5. Ron is the owner of a residential design firm in a state requiring interior designers to be licensed. His state also requires designers to have a separate license as a contractor if they sell

architectural products, cabinets, and built-ins. He is a member of an interior design professional association.

He was hired by a client to redesign the kitchen and family room. The design concept he recommended required moving the locations of the sink and refrigerator—which had an icemaker. Ron also specified new cabinets, lighting fixtures, flooring, and wall tile. The client purchased everything except granite countertops and ceramic tile for the walls and floors from Ron.

When the client received an invoice from Ron for the work, she questioned a line item called "special fees" as well as the prices for the wall tile and lighting fixtures. He claimed the "special fees" charge was his fee to supervise all the work and was in addition to his design fee. The client thought the special fees charge was improper and refused to pay it. She also wondered why Ron billed her for the wall tile. Ron emailed the client that if she didn't pay the invoice as billed, he would stop the other work that was still ongoing at the house. The client emailed back that she was contacting her attorney as well as planning to file an ethics complaint against Ron.

- Review the case, and detail facts concerning the issue. Don't forget to also list questions you have regarding any missing information.

- Determine if Ron has in fact violated any part of an association's code of ethics. Defend your decision.

6. Arthur had been working for the past three months with a client, Mr. Jones, to design his office suite. Mr. Jones was a friend of Arthur's accountant, who had recommended the designer to Jones. Everything was going well until the installation of wall coverings and cabinets in the office. Mr. Jones mentioned to the wallpaper installer that the paper was

not what he had selected and told him to stop the installation. The installer stopped the work and tried to contact the designer. Jones also called, left a message on Arthur's answering machine, and emailed Arthur to tell him about the problem. The next day the cabinet company was scheduled to install the cabinets but could not do so unless the walls were finished.

Arthur did not immediately respond to Mr. Jones or the installer, as he was at another appointment and didn't get the message. His phone was not working properly and he did not see the email until he returned to the office. The client was getting upset about the problems with the installations, as he wanted to get moved in over the weekend.

Mr. Jones sent another email and made another phone call to Arthur the next day but still received no response. When Arthur finally contacted Jones by email—three days later—he told him in part that Mr. Jones should not have told the installer to stop working, as it wasn't his prerogative to do so. He said he would look into it and get back to Jones. The client emailed Arthur that it was critical that everything be taken care of immediately, since he needed to move into the office space tomorrow. Arthur went out of town for the weekend and did not return the email or phone Jones for another two days.

■ Is there an ethical issue involved with this case as it has been described?

■ If you were Arthur, what would you do to resolve the situation?

7. Sally bragged to you that she received an "extra special discount" from a vendor for specifying products for a hospital project in a small town. The extra discount wasn't actually a reduced price for the goods; it was, in fact, a free weekend at

a prestigious resort for Sally and a guest. Sally would have to pay for transportation to the resort since it was out of state; all the other expenses would be paid by the vendor.

Sally specified those products, and the hospital subsequently purchased everything from Sally's firm.

■ Is there an ethical issue in this case?

8. Elizabeth is an interior designer who knew the client, Mr. Olsen, from a charitable group to which they both belonged. Although he had previously asked her to design his office, she refused, saying that she did not have the expertise to do a proper job. She did not recommend anyone, but suggested he contact the association referral service for some names.

A few months later Mr. Olsen contacted Elizabeth to ask her opinion on some products that had been installed in his office. He was unhappy with the quality of the products and the workmanship of the custom cabinets. Since he knew Elizabeth, he wondered if she could look at the office and voice an opinion. Elizabeth agreed to do this because she personally did not know the designer who had done the work.

■ Is there an ethics issue here? Discuss what you think Elizabeth should do.

9. Jessica and Philip are partners in a design practice and have worked together for over 10 years. Both are licensed and members of a professional association. Their practice specializes in high-end residential properties in a large metropolitan city. Philip also obtains professional office space projects, especially for attorneys, doctors, and other professionals. They collaborate on projects, though the lead designer for each project is the one who brings in the project.

Philip obtained a residential project from a client, Mr. Johnson, who had Philip design his law office two years ago. Because of his workload, Philip asked Jessica to help out, but he would remain lead designer.

The scope of services called for a complete design, specification, and the procurement of any needed products. Philip informed the client that some architectural changes might be needed and that he would work with the client's architect on those changes. The client agreed to a flat fee for services plus a markup on any merchandise or other products sold by Jessica and Philip's company.

The project was going essentially well, except that Mr. Johnson's wife was constantly inserting herself into decisions and making changes in the plans and product specifications. She said she found some better products on the Internet and wanted to use those instead of what the designers had recommended. This meant that the project was taking longer than the original estimate.

Jessica's workload with the Johnsons had increased significantly beyond her original expectation when Philip became very involved with several office projects. Jessica utilized an intern to help with communications with the client and to take care of other tasks for the Johnson residence.

When the furniture and other items were delivered, Mrs. Johnson became very upset that the fabric on seating and the finish on the pieces for the dining room and master bedroom were not what had been agreed to.

Philip met with the Johnsons. He showed them the samples and sign-off sheets that Jessica had obtained for the furniture. Mrs. Johnson was adamant about the "wrong things" being delivered and that she wanted them removed and replaced with the right furniture items.

- Review the case and determine if any ethics violations exist.

- Describe how you would resolve this situation as if you were Philip so that:
  - The clients are satisfied.
  - The design firm does not lose a good client.
  - The design firm receives fair compensation.

NOTES

1. Roger LeRoy Miller and Gaylord A. Jentz, *Business Law Today: The Essentials,* 7th ed. (Mason, OH: Thomson, 2006), 47.
2. Gordon Marshall, *A Dictionary of Sociology,* 2nd ed. (New York: Oxford University Press, 1998), 527.
3. Robert W. Kolb, ed., *Encyclopedia of Business Ethics and Society,* Vol. 2 (Thousand Oaks, CA: Sage, 2008), 778.
4. Gordon W. Brown and Paul A. Sukys, *Business Law with UCC Applications,* 9th ed. (New York: Glencoe/McGraw-Hill, 1997), 8–9.

References

Abramowitz, Ava J. 2002. *Architect's Essentials of Contract Negotiation*. Hoboken, NJ: John Wiley & Sons.

American Institute of Architects. 2007. *Design for Aging Post-Occupancy Evaluations*. Hoboken, NJ: John Wiley & Sons.

American Society of Interior Designers. *Code of Ethics and Professional Conduct*. Available online at www.asid.org.

Andolina, Michael. 2001. *Critical Thinking for Working Students*. Albany, NY: Delmar/Thomson Learning.

Babcock, Linda, and Sara Laschever. 2003. *Women Don't Ask. Negotiation and the Gender Divide*. Princeton, NJ: Princeton University Press.

Beach, Lee Roy. 1997. *The Psychology of Decision Making*. Thousand Oaks, CA: Sage.

Becker, Franklin. Closing the Research-Design Gap. *Implications* 5(10). Informdesign.com, no date, pp. 1–5.

Berens, Michael. 2008. Using Research in Design Practice. *ASID ICON*, September/October: 30–31.

Berger, Warren. 2009. *Glimmer: How Design Can Transform Your Life, and Maybe Even the World*. New York: Penguin Press.

Bird, Polly. 2010. *Improve Your Time Management*. New York: McGraw-Hill.

Booth, Wayne C., Gregory G. Colomb, and Joseph M. Williams. 2008. *The Craft of Research*, 3rd ed. Chicago: University of Chicago Press.

Bowden, Mark. 2010. *Winning Body Language*. New York: McGraw-Hill.

Bowles, Michelle. 2009. The Power to Deliver. *IIDA Perspective*, Summer: 15–20.

Brodow, Ed. 2006. *Negotiation Boot Camp*. New York: Currency Books/Doubleday.

Brown, Gordon W., and Paul A. Sukys. 1997. *Business Law with UCC Applications*, 9th ed. New York: Glencoe/McGraw-Hill.

Brown, Tim. 2009. *Change by Design*. New York: HarperCollins.

Brown, Tim. 2008. Design Thinking. *Harvard Business Review*, June: 84–92.

Brown, Tim, and Jocelyn Wyatt. 2010. Design Thinking for Social Innovation. *Stanford Social Innovation Review* 8(1): 30–35.

Browne, M. Neil, and Stuart M. Keeley. 2007. *Asking the Right Questions*, 7th ed. Upper Saddle River, NJ: Pearson/Prentice Hall.

Browne, M. Neil and Stuart M. Keeley. 2010. *Asking the Right Questions*, 9th ed. Upper Saddle River, NJ: Pearson/Prentice Hall.

Brunner, Robert, and Steward Emery, with Russ Hall. 2009. *Do You Matter? How Great Design Will Make People Love Your Company*. Upper Saddle River, NJ: FT Press.

Burley-Allen, Madelyn. 1995. *Listening: The Forgotten Skill*, 2nd ed. New York: John Wiley & Sons.

Cama, Rosalyn. 2009. *Evidence-Based Healthcare Design*. Hoboken, NJ: John Wiley & Sons.

The Center for Health Design/Evidence-Based Design Accreditation and Certification. www.healthdesign.org/edac.

Ching, Frances D. K., and Corky Binggeli. 2004. *Interior Design Illustrated*, 2nd ed. Hoboken, NJ: John Wiley & Sons.

Cohen, Herb. 1980. *You Can Negotiate Anything*. New York: Bantam Books.

Collins, Denis. 2009. *Essentials of Business Ethics*. Hoboken, NJ: John Wiley & Sons.

Collins, John W. III, and Nancy Patricia O'Brien, eds. 2003. *The Greenwood Dictionary of Education*. Westport, CT: Greenwood Press.

Cusick, William J. 2009. *All Customers Are Irrational*. New York: American Management Association.

Davies, Nikolas, and Erkki Jokiniemi. 2008. *Dictionary of Architecture and Building Construction*. Burlington, MA: Architectural Press/Elsevier.

Delmar, Ken. 1984. *Winning Moves: The Body Language of Selling*. New York: Warner Books.

Demkin, Joseph A., executive ed. 2008. *Architect's Handbook of Professional Practice*. 14th ed. Hoboken, NJ: John Wiley & Sons.

Dess, Gregory G., G. T. Lumpkin, and Marilyn L. Taylor. 2004. *Strategic Management: Text and Cases*. Boston: McGraw-Hill/Irwin.

Dickinson, Joan I., Lori Anthony, and John P. Marsden. 2009. Faculty Perceptions Regarding Research: Are We on the Right Track?" *Journal of Interior Design* 35(1): 1–14.

Dickinson, Joan I., John P. Marsden, and Marilyn A. Read. 2007. Empirical Design Research: Student Definitions, Perceptions, and Values. *Journal of Interior Design* 32(2): 1–16.

Dohr, Joy, Denise Guerin, and Kate Bukoski. n.d. Research 101: An On-line Tutorial. *Implications* 2(1): 1–4. InformeDesign.com.

Doppelt, Bob. 2008. *The Power of Sustainable Thinking*. London: Earthscan.

Eakins, Patricia. 2005. *Writing for Interior Design*. New York: Fairchild Books.

Elvin, George. 2007. *Integrated Practice in Architecture*. Hoboken, NJ: John Wiley & Sons.

Esty, Daniel C., and Andrew S. Winston. 2006. *Green to Gold! How Smart Companies Use Environmental Strategy to Innovate, Create Value, and Build Competitive Advantage*. New Haven, CT: Yale University Press.

Fadem, Terry J. 2009. *The Art of Asking*. Upper Saddle River, NJ: Pearson Education.

Fast, Julius. 1970. *Body Language*. New York: Pocket Books.

Fisher, Roger, William Ury, and Bruce Patton. 1991. *Getting to Yes*, 2nd ed. New York: Houghton Mifflin.

Freese, Thomas. 2003. *Secrets of Question Based Selling*. Naperville, IL: Sourcebooks.

Geboy, Lyn, and Amy Beth Keller. n.d. Research in Practice: The Design Researchers' Perspective." *Implications* 4(11): 1–7. Informedesign.com.

Gitman, Lawrence J., and Carl McDaniel. 2003. *The Best of the Future of Business*. Mason, OH: Thomson/Southwest.

Gladwell, Malcolm. 2005. *Blink: The Power of Thinking without Thinking*. New York: Little Brown.

Gomez-Mejia, Luis R., David B. Balkin, and Robert L. Cardy. 2005. *Management*, 2nd ed. New York: McGraw-Hill.

Goulston, Mark. 2010. *Just Listen. Discover the Secret to Getting Through to Absolutely Anyone*. New York: American Management Association.

Gove, Philip Babcock, ed. 1993. *Webster's Third New International Dictionary.* Springfield, MA: Merriam-Webster.

Groat, Linda, and David Wang. 2002. *Architectural Research Methods.* Hoboken, NJ: John Wiley & Sons.

Halpern, Diane F. 2003. *Thought and Knowledge. An Introduction to Critical Thinking,* 4th ed. Mahwah, NJ: Lawrence Erlbaum.

Hamilton, D. Kirk, and David H. Watkins. 2009. *Evidence-Based Design for Multiple Building Types.* Hoboken, NJ: John Wiley & Sons.

Hamlin, Sonya. 2006. *How to Talk So People Listen.* New York: Harper.

Hammond, John S., Ralph L. Keeny, and Howard Raiffa. 2002. *Smart Choices: A Practical Guide to Making Better Decisions.* New York: Random House.

Harvard Business Review. 2001. *The Harvard Business Review on Decision Making,* 6th ed. Cambridge, MA: Harvard Business School Press.

Harvard Business Review. 2000. *Harvard Business Review on Negotiation and Conflict Resolution.* Cambridge, MA: Harvard Business School Press.

Heyman, Richard. 1994. *Why Didn't You Say That in the First Place?* San Francisco: Jossey-Bass/Wiley.

Hill, Napoleon. (Edited by Bill Hartley and Ann Hartley). 2004. *Think and Grow Rich,* 21st century ed. Los Angeles, CA: Highroads Media.

Hindes, Steve. 2005. *Think for Yourself!* Golden, CO: Fulcrum.

Howe, Neil, and William Strauss. 2000. *Millennials Rising: The Next Great Generation.* New York: Vintage Books/Random House.

Hurson, Tim. 2008. *Think Better.* New York: McGraw-Hill.

International Interior Design Association. *Code of Ethics.* Available online at www.iida.org.

Jennings, Marianne M. 2006. *Business Ethics,* 5th ed. Mason, OH: Thomson.

Johnson, Spenser. 1992. *"Yes" or "No": The Guide to Better Decisions.* New York: HarperCollins.

Kaplinger, Eunice, and Susan Ray-Degges. 1998. Can Ethics Be Taught or Is It Too Late? *Journal of Interior Design* 24(1): 48–54.

Karlen, Mark. 2004. *Space Planning Basics,* 2nd ed. Hoboken, NJ: John Wiley & Sons.

Kerzner, Harold. 2003. *Project Management: A Systems Approach to Planning, Scheduling, and Controlling,* 8th ed. Hoboken, NJ: John Wiley & Sons.

Kilmer, Rosemary, and W. Otie Kilmer. 1992. *Designing Interiors*. Fort Worth, TX: Harcourt Brace Jovanovich.

Kolb, Robert W., ed. 2008. *Encyclopedia of Business Ethics and Society*. (5 volumes). Thousand Oaks, CA: Sage.

Leonard, Dorothy, and Jeffrey F. Rayport. 1997. Spark Innovation Through Empathic Design. *Harvard Business Review*, November–December: 102–112.

Lehrer, Jonah. 2009. *How We Decide*. Boston: Houghton Mifflin/Harcourt.

Leibold, Marius, Gilbert J. B. Probst, and Michael Gibbert. 2002. *Strategic Management in the Knowledge Economy*. Hoboken, NJ: John Wiley & Sons.

Lieberman, David J. 2007. *You Can Read Anyone*. New York: MJF Books.

Lockwood, Thomas, ed. 2010. *Design Thinking*. New York: Allworth Press.

Long, Deborah H. 2000. *Ethics and the Design Professions*. Washington, DC: National Council for Interior Design Qualification.

Long, Deborah H. 1998. Why We Need Ethical Decision-Making Skills. *ASID Professional Designer*, May/June: 19–23.

Luntz, Frank. 2007. *Words that Work*. New York: Hyperion.

MacKenzie, Alec, and Pat Nickerson. 2009. *The Time Trap*, 4th ed. New York: American Management Association.

Marquardt, Michael. 2005. *Leading with Questions*. New York: Jossey-Bass.

Marshall, Gordon. 1998. *A Dictionary of Sociology*, 2nd ed. New York: Oxford University Press.

Martin, Caren. 2008. Rebuttal of the Report by the Institute of Justice Entitled Designing Cartels: How Industry Insiders Cut Out Competition. *Journal of Interior Design*. 3(3): 1–49.

Martin, Roger. 2009. *The Design of Business*. Cambridge, MA: Harvard University Press.

Maruska, Don. 2004. *How Great Decisions Are Made*. New York: American Management Association.

McKay, Matthew, Martha Davis, and Patrick Fanning. 1995. *How to Communicate*, 2nd ed. New York: Barnes & Noble Books.

McGowan, Mary Rose, and Kelly Kruse. 2004. *Interior Graphic Standards*, Student edition. Hoboken, NJ: John Wiley & Sons.

McKean, Erin, ed. 2005. *The New Oxford American Dictionary*, 2nd ed. New York: Oxford University Press.

Miller, Roger LeRoy, and Gaylord A. Jentz. 2006. *Business Law Today: the Essentials*, 7th ed. Mason, OH: Thomson.

MindTools. 2010. What If Analysis. www.mindtools.com.

Moore, Brooke Noel, and Richard Parker. 2004. *Critical Thinking*. New York: McGraw-Hill.

Morgenstern, Julie. 2004. *Time Management from the Inside Out*, 2nd ed. New York: Henry Holt & Co.

Nadler, Gerald, and William J. Chandon. 2004. *Smart Questions*. New York: Jossey-Bass.

Navarro, Joe, with Toni Sciarra Poynter. 2010. *Louder Than Words*. New York: Harper Business.

Neumeier, Marty. 2009. *The Designful Company*. Berkeley, CA: New Riders.

Nierenberg, Gerard I. 1996. *The Art of Creative Thinking*. New York: Barnes & Noble Press.

Nierenberg, Gerard I., and Henry H. Calero. 2009. *The New Art of Negotiating*. Garden City, NY: Square One.

———. 1971. *How to Read a Person Like a Book*. New York: Pocket Books.

Nussbaumer, Linda L. 2009. *Evidence-Based Design for Interior Designers*. New York: Fairchild Books.

Osterwalder, Alexander, and Yves Pigneur. 2010. *Business Model Generation*, Hoboken, NJ: John Wiley & Sons.

The Oxford American College Dictionary. 2002. New York: Oxford University Press.

Pack, Thomas. 1997. *10 Minute Guide to Business Research on the Internet*. Indianapolis, IN.: Que/Macmillan.

Palmer, Stephanie. 2008. *Good in a Room*. New York: Currency/Doubleday.

Patterson, Kerry, Joseph Grenny, David Maxfield, Ron McMillan, and Al Switzler. 2008. *Influencer: The Power to Change Anything*. New York: McGraw-Hill.

Patterson, Kerry, Joseph Grenny, Ron McMillan, and Al Switzler. 2002. *Crucial Conversations: Tools for Talking When Stakes Are High*. New York: McGraw-Hill.

Paul, Richard W., and Linda Elder. 2002. *Critical Thinking*. Upper Saddle River, NJ: Pearson Education.

Pease, Allan, and Barbara Pease. 2006. *The Definitive Book of Body Language*. New York: Bantam Books.

Peña, William M., and Steven A. Parshall. 2001. *Problem Seeking*, 4th ed. New York: John Wiley & Sons.

Perkins, P. S. 2008. *The Art and Science of Communication*. Hoboken, NJ: John Wiley & Sons.

Pile, John. 1995. *Interior Design*, 2nd ed. Englewood Cliffs, NJ: Prentice-Hall.

Piotrowski, Christine M. 2008. *Professional Practice for Interior Designers*, 4th ed. Hoboken, NJ: John Wiley & Sons.

Preiser, Wolfgang F. E., Harvey Z. Rabinowitz, and Edward T. White. 1988. *Post-Occupancy Evaluation*. New York: Van Nostrand Reinhold.

Reck, Ross R., and Brian G. Long. 1987. *The Win-Win Negotiator*. Kalamazoo, MI: Spartan.

Reichenbach, Bruce R. 2001. *Introduction to Critical Thinking*. Boston: McGraw-Hill.

Roam, Dan. 2008. *The Back of the Napkin. Solving Problems and Selling Ideas With Pictures*. New York: Portfolio/Penguin.

Rosen, Evan. 2007. *The Culture of Collaboration*. San Francisco, CA: Red Ape.

Rosenblum, Lawrence D. 2010. *See What I'm Saying: The Extraordinary Powers of Our Five Senses*. New York: Norton.

Ruchlis, Hy, with Sandra Oddo. 1990. *Clear Thinking*. Amherst, NY: Prometheus Books.

Saunders, Mark, Philip Lewis, and Adrian Thornhill. 2003. *Research Methods for Business Students*, 3rd ed. Essex, UK: Pearson/Prentice-Hall.

Sawyer, Keith. 2007. *Group Genius: The Creative Power of Collaboration*. Cambridge, MA: Basic Books/Perseus.

Schwab, Donald P. 1999. *Research Methods for Organizational Studies*. Mahwah, NJ: Lawrence Erlbaum.

Scott, Susan. 2002. *Fierce Conversations*. New York: Berkley Books.

Shiveley, James M., and Phillip J. VanFossen. 2001. *Using Internet Primary Sources to Teach Critical Thinking Skills in Government, Economics, and Contemporary World Issues*. Westport, CT: Greenwood Press.

Shore, Zachary. 2008. *Blunder: Why Smart People Make Bad Decisions*. New York: Bloomsbury.

Simons, Tony. 2008. *The Integrity Divide*. New York: Jossey-Bass/Wiley.

Surveymonkey.com. An organization that will assist businesses in obtaining a wide variety of information through the use of online surveys.

Tischler, Linda. 2009. IDEO's David Kelley on Design Thinking. www.Fastcompany.com, January 14.

Tracy, Brian. 2007. *The Art of Closing the Sale*. Nashville, TN: Thomas Nelson.

Tulgan, Bruce. 2009. *Not Everyone Gets a Trophy: How to Manage Generation Y*. San Francisco: Jossey-Bass/Wiley.

Underhill, Paco. 1999. *Why We Buy: The Science of Shopping*. New York: Simon & Schuster.

VanGundy, Arthur B. 2007. *Getting into Innovation*. New York: American Management Association.

Verganti, Roberto. 2009. *Design-Driven Innovation*. Cambridge, MA: Harvard University Press.

Wand, Kelley, ed. 2009. *White-Collar Crime*. Detroit, MI: GALE/CENG Age Learning.

Wang, David. 2007. Diagramming Design Research. *Journal of Interior Design* 33(1): 33–43.

Walsh, Richard. 2008. *Time Management*, 2nd ed. Avon, MA: Adams Business.

Wasserman, Barry, Patrick J. Sullivan, and Gregory Palermo. 2000. *Ethics and the Practice of Architecture*. New York: John Wiley & Sons.

Watanabe, Ken. 2009. *Problem Solving 101*. New York: Portfolio/Penguin Books.

WBDG Aesthetics Subcommittee. 2010. Engage the Integrated Design Process. *WBDG—Whole Building Design Guide*. June 4. www.wbdg.org/design.

Welch, David. 2002. *Decisions, Decisions*. Amherst, NY: Prometheus Books.

Weston, Anthony. 2007. *Creativity for Critical Thinkers*. New York: Oxford University Press.

Wyllys, R. E. January 2003. Systematic Inquiry and New Knowledge. School of Information, The University of Texas at Austin. www.ischool.utexas.edu.

Zikmund, William G. 1994. *Business Research Methods*, 4th ed. Fort Worth, TX: Dryden Press/Harcourt Brace College.

Zimring, Craig, Mahbub Rashid, and Kevin Kampschroer. 2010. Facility Performance Evaluation (FPE). *Whole Building Design Guide*. June 11. www.wbdg.org.

Index